SPLENDID LOW-CARBING for Life (vol-1)

Another Splendid Guide for Low-Carbing
By Jennifer Eloff

Author of National Best-selling Cookbooks

Splendid Low-Carbing and *More Splendid Low-Carbing*

Splendid Desserts and *More Splendid Desserts*

Canadian Cataloguing in Publication Data
Eloff, Jennifer, 1957
Splendid Low-Carbing for Life (vol-1)
First Printing ~ October 2003

ISBN 0-7795-0047-4   Includes Index.
1. Low-carb diet recipes. 2. Sugarless recipes.
3. Desserts, cooking and baking low-carb recipes.
4.   Title 5. Another Splendid Guide for Low-Carbing.

Inspiration: Thank you God from the bottom of my heart!

Photography: Ian Eloff and Ross Hutchinson
Front and Back Cover Design: Ian and Jonathan Eloff
Web-site Enhancements: Daniel and Ian Eloff
Printed in Calgary, Canada by **Blitzprint** (www.Blitzprint.com)

Pictured on front cover: Aunty Marie's Blueberry Muffins, Pineapple Raspberry Muffins, Cranberry Orange Loaf, Apple Spice Loaf, & Strawberry and Vanilla Meal Replacement Shakes

Pictured on back cover: Mini Hot Chocolate Cake, Deluxe Chocolate Chip Cookies, Cream Cheese Bran Waffle, Pumpkin Spice Loaf & Hazelnut Chocolate Bundt Cake

Published by **Eureka Publishing**

Copyright © Jennifer Eloff, 2003

CONTENTS

HELPFUL HINTS

1.   Some information about **SPLENDA®** **Brand Sweetener**: The granular version is used cup-for-cup as you would sugar. The caloric and carbohydrate content is:

> 1 tsp (5 mL)   =   2 calories, *0.5 g carbs*
>
> 1 cup (250 mL) =   96 calories, *24.0 g carbs*
>
> SPLENDA® packets: 1 packet is the equivalent of 2 tsp (10 mL) sugar.
>
> 1 packet = 4 calories, *0.9 g carbs* (say, 1 gram, for ease of calculation)

I've discovered that, in certain recipes, it is possible to substitute 8 SPLENDA® packets (*8 g carbs*) instead of 24 packets (*24 g carbs*) for 1 cup (250 mL) SPLENDA® Granular (*24 g carbs*). That is a reduction in carbs by two thirds. Typically, I've utilized this option in some confections and puddings and a few other recipes. The only drawback, of course, is having to open all those packets! The results can be a little less predictable in baking, and I still think SPLENDA® Granular is the best option for that purpose.

2. It is easy to replace SPLENDA® Granular (and reduce carbs) with **Da Vinci®** **Sugar Free Syrup**, where there is already liquid such as water or cream used in creating the recipe, that can be replaced.   It is also possible to use other brands of sugar free syrups, however, I do prefer Da Vinci® Syrups as they are primarily sweetened with sucralose (no carbs or calories). One can substitute SPLENDA® Granular with any other granulated sweetener that is suitable for baking. If liquid SPLENDA® (pure sucralose in solution) becomes available, this too may be used instead of the granular sweetener. Sugar free Kool-Aid® or flavored extracts, water and SPLENDA® Granular may be used instead of sugar free syrups.

3. All flavors of Da Vinci® Gourmet Sugar Free Syrup may be purchased online at www.davincigourmet.com.   United Grocers Cash and Carry in the U.S.A. carries these syrups at wholesale prices. Walmart stores carry some as well. Guar gum, xanthan gum, Bob's Red Mill vital wheat gluten (my breads typically require this product for best results) and sugar free chocolate chips, among many other products, are available from http://stores.yahoo.com/carbsmart/.Whole milk powder can be obtained from www.americanspice.com (click on "powders" and then click on "show all" on the page that appears). www.bobsredmill.com and

www.synergydiet.com have specialty low-carb products. Most of the specialty ingredients for the recipes may be purchased at upscale health food stores or grocery stores with a large health food section. An excellent site with research and links to online stores as well is: http://www.lowcarbsuccess.net/

4. **Thickening Agent**, page 57, is something I utilize frequently throughout the cookbook, however, if you would like the convenience of a commercial product, then use "ThickenThin not/Starch" by Expert Foods (http://expertfoods.com).

5. Large **eggs** were used, unless otherwise specified.

6. **Net Carbs:** The nutritional analysis for each recipe shows the carbohydrates with the fiber already subtracted. See Book 1 for an explanation.

7. In this cookbook I've explored using **flavored whey protein powders** (not isolate). Costco sells an inexpensive vanilla-flavored sucralose-sweetened brand.

8. **Ultimate Bake Mixes** - Substitute your choice of Ultimate Bake Mix, page 67, even a nut-free one, page 68, if desired, despite the fact that a recipe calls for a particular one (means it was tested with that one). Slight differences occur in the baked products and nutritional analysis. Vital Ultimate Bake Mixes are my favorite, as they produce great-tasting, moist baked goods. Leftover bake mix can be added to at a later date or used in a variety of ways: add seasoning to bake mix and "flour" meat, chicken, fish or veggies before frying. I store my bake mixes in containers at room temperature, however they may be refrigerated.

9. **Unsweetened chocolate** that is frequently used in recipes is the garden-variety baker's chocolate without any sweetener. Sugar free chocolate is often sweetened with maltitol, which is a sugar alcohol that cannot be eaten in excess, without causing a laxative effect. Ross® bars seem less problematic. These are available online at http://www.synergydiet.com/chocolates.html.

10. There are a few recipes that reference other recipes from my previous low-carb cookbooks; however, I've included several of those more frequently used recipes in the **Miscellaneous** section, for your convenience.

DEDICATION: This book took approximately 6 months to create, edit and get ready for publishing. It was a labor of love, and I hope you'll find some recipes that will make your low-carb life easier and more enjoyable, as they have ours. Once again, I thank God very humbly for giving me the inspiration, talent and determination to see this project and previous ones through. My almost nightly prayer for many years was for my Father in heaven to enable me to help others, and I believe that prayer was answered mightily. I feel blessed to serve people in this manner. Thanks also go to my dear family for their love and support.

BEVERAGES

RASPBERRY ICED TEA

Refreshing! Serve over crushed ice or add ice to the drink.

3 regular tea bags, OR herbal tea bags,
 raspberry-flavored
1 cup boiling water (250 mL)
1½ cups ice cold water (375 mL)
1½ cups Da Vinci® Sugar (375 mL)
 Free Raspberry Syrup
1 tsp lemon juice (5 mL)

> **Yield:** 4 cups (1 L)
> 1 cup (250 mL) per serving
> 0.9 calories
> 0.0 g protein
> 0.0 g fat
> ***0.3 g carbs***

In medium saucepan, place tea bags in boiling water; leave in 5 minutes. Remove tea bags. Pour tea into 4-cup (1L) juice jug. Add ice cold water, Da Vinci® Sugar Free Raspberry Syrup and lemon juice. Stir well. Refrigerate.

Variations: **Create-a-Flavor Iced Tea:** Use any flavor Da Vinci® Sugar Free Syrup to create different iced teas all summer long.

Da Vinci® Alternative: Use sugar free Kool-Aid® and SPLENDA® Granular to flavor the iced tea to taste.

ITALIAN BLUEBERRY VANILLA SODA

Create your own combinations too. I owe this recipe to my dear husband.

1 tbsp Da Vinci® Sugar Free (15 mL)
 Blueberry Syrup
1 tbsp Da Vinci® Sugar Free (15 mL)
 Vanilla Syrup
1 tsp whipping cream, OR to taste (5 mL)
1 cup carbonated water (250 mL)

> **Yield:** 1 serving
> 1 serving
> 16.1 calories
> 0.1 g protein
> 1.7 g fat
> ***0.1 g carbs***

In cold glass, combine Da Vinci® Sugar Free Blueberry and Vanilla Syrups. Stir in cream. Add carbonated water.

MEAL REPLACEMENT SHAKE

This delicious shake may be used occasionally in place of a meal, or on the Fat Fast, or to help induce ketosis. Make sure to take your supplements, including potassium, calcium, magnesium and plenty of water, to protect electrolyte balance in the body. Lovely served with a dollop of Crème Fraiche.

Chocolate Shake:
$^3/_4$ cup ice cold water (175 mL)
$^1/_2$ cup whipping cream (125 mL)
$^1/_2$ cup Da Vinci® Sugar Free (125 mL)
  Chocolate Syrup
$^1/_2$ cup Da Vinci® Sugar Free (125 mL)
  Pancake Syrup
$^1/_2$ cup chocolate whey protein (125 mL)
1 large egg
$1^1/_2$ tbsp olive oil (22 mL)
1 tbsp Dutch cocoa (15 mL)
1 SPLENDA® packet, (optional)
$^1/_2$ tsp Thickening Agent, (optional) (2 mL)

Yield: 3 cups (750 mL) 1 cup (250 mL) per serving 254.9 calories 11.9 g protein 22.0 g fat ***3.0 g carbs***

In blender, add water, whipping cream, Da Vinci® Sugar Free Chocolate Syrup and Da Vinci® Sugar Free Pancake Syrup, chocolate whey protein, egg, olive oil, Dutch cocoa, SPLENDA® and Thickening Agent, if using; blend well.

Variations: **Create-a-Flavor Shake:** Use any flavor of whey protein and Da Vinci® Sugar Free Syrup to flavor your shake. Omit cocoa powder, where necessary, and use 1 tbsp (15 mL) whole or skim milk powder instead, if desired, or omit it. These changes will result in a slight increase in carbs: (***3.8 g Carbs***).

Vanilla Shake: Use vanilla whey protein, Da Vinci® Sugar Free Vanilla or French Vanilla Syrup and 1 tbsp (15 mL) whole or skim milk powder. Omit cocoa.

Strawberry Shake: Use strawberry whey protein, Da Vinci® Sugar Free Strawberry Syrup and 1 tbsp (15 mL) whole or skim milk powder. Omit cocoa.

Raspberry Shake: Use raspberry whey protein, Da Vinci® Sugar Free Raspberry Syrup and 1 tbsp (15 mL) whole or skim milk powder. Omit cocoa.

Raspberry Chocolate Shake: Use chocolate whey protein, cocoa and Da Vinci® Sugar Free Raspberry Syrup.

Helpful Hint: Thickening Agent, page 57, added makes a slightly thicker shake, however, it cuts the sweetness somewhat; therefore, add the extra SPLENDA® suggested.

FROZEN STRAWBERRY LEMON PUNCH

This punch is absolutely delicious and easy to prepare!

$1^1/_2$ cups Da Vinci® Sugar Free (375 mL)
  Strawberry or Raspberry Syrup
$^3/_4$ cup lemon juice from (175 mL)
  concentrate (or fresh squeezed)
2 cups frozen strawberries, (500 mL)
  unsweetened (about 10 oz {300 g})
$^1/_2$ cup SPLENDA® Granular (125 mL)
8 cups ice cold carbonated water (2 L)

> **Yield:** 24 servings
> $^1/_2$ cup (125 mL) per serving
> 9.0 calories
> 0.1 g protein
> 0.0 g fat
> **2.2 g carbs**

In blender, blend Da Vinci® Sugar Free Strawberry or Raspberry Syrup, lemon juice, frozen strawberries and SPLENDA® Granular. Refrigerate until serving time.

Pour juice concentrate into punch bowl, just before serving. Add carbonated water and stir gently. Garnish each glass with a slice of lemon, if desired.

CHAI SPICE MIX

I enjoy Chai tea quite often using this mix. I don't even bother to strain it (extra fiber!). It reminds me of having a cup of hot chocolate.

$^1/_2$ cup whole milk powder, OR (125 mL)
  skim milk powder*
$^1/_2$ cup SPLENDA® Granular (125 mL)
$1^1/_2$ tsp cinnamon (7 mL)
1 tsp ground ginger (5 mL)
$^1/_4$ tsp nutmeg (1 mL)
$^1/_4$ tsp allspice (1 mL)
$^1/_8$ tsp ground cloves (0.5 mL)

> **Yield:** 1 cup (250 mL)
> 1 tsp (5 mL) per serving
> 8.1 calories
> 0.4 g protein
> 0.4 g fat
> **0.9 g carbs**

In small bowl, combine whole milk or skim milk powder, SPLENDA® Granular, cinnamon, ginger, nutmeg, allspice and ground cloves. Add 1 tsp (5 mL) to 1 tbsp (15 mL) to a cup of hot tea or coffee, or add to a pot of tea or coffee, to taste. Strain tea or coffee, while pouring into cup from tea or coffee pot, if desired.

Helpful Hint: *If using skim milk powder, grind finely in blender.

APPETIZERS

TERIYAKI SCALLOP RUMAKI

A popular appetizer.

$^1/_2$ lb sea scallops (0.227 kg)
$^3/_4$ lb sliced bacon (0.340 kg)
Teriyaki Marinade:
3 tbsp soy sauce (45 mL)
3 tbsp SPLENDA® Granular (45 mL)
1 tbsp water (15 mL)
1 tsp ground ginger (5 mL)
$^1/_2$ tsp garlic powder (2 mL)
$^1/_4$ tsp Thickening Agent, page 57 (1 mL)

Yield: 6 servings
1 serving
145.0 calories
20.3 g protein
5.1 g fat
3.4 g carbs

Place scallops in glass pie dish.

Teriyaki Marinade: In small bowl, combine soy sauce, SPLENDA® Granular, water, ground ginger, garlic powder and Thickening Agent, page 57.

Pour marinade over scallops. Marinate half an hour, turning to coat scallops well.

Cut bacon strips horizontally in half and if they are very wide slices of bacon, cut down center as well. Wrap scallops snugly with bacon and fasten with wooden toothpicks.

Place on cookie sheet and bake in 375°F (190°C) oven 15 minutes, or until bacon is cooked.

Variations: Use whole, canned water chestnuts or fresh shrimp, shelled and deveined, instead of scallops.

MEXICAN TORTILLA ROLL-UPS

One of my favorite appetizers as well as my son, Jonathan's favorite! If desired, use a few, chopped, canned jalapenos instead of green chilies.

8 oz light cream cheese, (250 g)
  softened
4.5 oz can chopped green chilies (127 mL)
  drained
$^1/_2$ cup grated Cheddar Cheese, (125 mL)
  (optional)
$^1/_3$ cup chopped green onions (75 mL)
$^1/_2$ tsp crushed garlic (2 mL)
8 Whey Tortillas, *Splendid Low-Carbing*,
  page 123, OR low-carb commercial ones

Yield: 8 servings
1 serving
147.6 calories
8.5 g protein
9.8 g fat
5.5 g carbs

In medium bowl, combine softened cream cheese, green chilies, grated Cheddar cheese (if using), finely chopped green onions and garlic. Cover each tortilla with cream cheese spread. Roll up each tortilla. Place tortillas on dinner plate and cover with plastic wrap. Refrigerate 2 hours or more. Slice into narrow pieces and serve with Salsa for dipping.

HOT SPINACH DIP

Super dip or spread that goes well with low-carb crackers and sliced English cucumbers. This is bound to be a favorite at a party.

1 tbsp butter (15 mL)
$^1/_3$ cup chopped onion (75 mL)
8 oz light cream cheese, softened (250 g)
$^3/_4$ cup mayonnaise (175 mL)
$^1/_4$ tsp garlic powder (1 mL)
$1^1/_2$ cups grated Cheddar cheese (375 mL)
10 oz frozen, chopped spinach, (300 g)
  thawed and squeezed to remove liquid
8 slices bacon, crisply cooked

Yield: 12 servings
1 serving
247.6 calories
10.0 g protein
22.2 g fat
2.0 g carbs

In small skillet, melt butter and sauté onions until soft and translucent. In food processor with sharp blade or in blender, process cream cheese, mayonnaise and garlic powder until smooth. In medium bowl, combine cream cheese mixture, Cheddar cheese and spinach. Spread evenly in 9-inch (23 cm) glass pie dish. Crumble bacon over top. Bake in 350°F (180°C) oven 15 minutes. Serve immediately.

CHICKEN STRIPS WITH MEXI-CALI DIP

Spicy chicken strips with a cool, creamy Mexican-style dip. Very good.

1 lb chicken breast halves, (0.454 kg)
  cut into thin strips
1 tbsp olive oil (15 mL)
2 tbsp hot pepper sauce (25 mL)
2 tsp butter (10 mL)
Mexi-Cali Dip:
$^3/_4$ cup sour cream (175 mL)
$^1/_4$ cup medium or mild Salsa (50 mL)
$^1/_4$ cup grated Cheddar cheese (50 mL)
1 green onion, chopped

Yield: 6 servings
1 serving
147.3 calories
19.1 g protein
6.6 g fat
2.0 g carbs

In large skillet, fry chicken strips in olive oil, stirring frequently, until chicken is lightly browned and cooked through, about 7 to 10 minutes. Add hot pepper sauce and butter right at the end and stir just until butter melts. Remove skillet from heat.

Mexi-Cali Dip: In medium bowl, combine sour cream, Salsa, cheese and green onion. Serve hot chicken with dip.

STUFFED MUSHROOMS

I sometimes serve this as a vegetable side dish.

25 medium-sized mushrooms, stems
  removed (reserve 8 mushroom stems)
8 oz cream cheese, (250 g)
  softened
$^1/_8$ tsp garlic powder (0.5 mL)
6 slices bacon
$^1/_2$ cup diced onion (125 mL)
$^1/_2$ cup grated Cheddar cheese (125 mL)

Yield: 25 mushrooms
1 mushroom
56.0 calories
3.3 g protein
4.2 g fat
1.2 g carbs

Wash mushrooms really well. Pat dry with paper towels. Remove stems. Chop 8 stems finely. In medium bowl, combine cream cheese and garlic powder. In skillet, cook bacon until crisp; remove and crumble over cream cheese. In bacon fat, stir-fry onion and mushroom stems until tender. Pour off excess fat. Add vegetables to cream cheese-bacon mixture; mix well. Stuff each mushroom and place on lightly greased cookie sheet. Sprinkle each mushroom with a little Cheddar cheese. Bake in 350°F (180°C) oven 15 minutes.

PECAN CHEESE RING
Pretty as a picture!

8 cups grated Cheddar cheese (2 L)
1 cup mayonnaise (250 mL)
1 tsp creamed horseradish (5 mL)
1 tsp prepared mustard (5 mL)
1 tsp cayenne pepper (5 mL)
1 cup chopped pecans (250 mL)
1 cup strawberry fruit spread, (250 mL)
  (optional)

Yield: 24 servings
1 serving
192.4 calories
10.3 g protein
16.4 g fat
1.2 g carbs

In large bowl, combine Cheddar cheese, mayonnaise, horseradish, mustard and cayenne pepper. Stir well. Place 3-inch custard cup in center of 9-inch (23 cm) springform pan. Sprinkle almost half the pecans in springform pan. Spread cheese mixture over top and smooth surface. Cover with plastic wrap.

Refrigerate until firm (about 2 hours). Place on pretty serving plate. Pat remaining pecans on top and around circumference of cheese ring. Surround with low-carb crackers and, if desired, spoon strawberry fruit spread in center.

SHRIMP STARTER
Elegant served in champagne glasses.

3 cups frozen cooked shrimp (750 mL)
$^3/_4$ cup chopped red pepper (175 mL)
3 green onions, chopped
$^1/_2$ cup mayonnaise (125 mL)
$^1/_4$ cup nonfat sour cream (50 mL)
$^1/_4$ tsp salt, or to taste (1 mL)
$^1/_4$ tsp mustard powder (1 mL)
$^1/_8$ tsp white pepper (0.5 mL)
3 cups leaf lettuce, rinsed (750 mL)

Yield: 6 servings
1 serving
244.1 calories
18.5 g protein
15.8 g fat
4.0 g carbs

In colander over large basin, rinse salad shrimp under running cold water until thawed. (Refrigerate at this point to chill shrimp until later, if desired) In medium bowl, combine well-drained shrimp, red pepper and green onions. In small bowl, combine mayonnaise, nonfat sour cream, salt, mustard powder and pepper; stir well. Pour over shrimp and mix well.

In 6 champagne glasses, arrange lettuce leaves and divide shrimp mixture evenly between them. Serve immediately.

AVOCADO MAYONNAISE DIP

Use this very tasty dip instead of mayonnaise as well. My good friend, Margaret Wolf, of Vernon, B.C. loved this dip.

$1^1/_2$ California avocadoes
$^1/_3$ cup olive oil (75 mL)
3 tbsp SPLENDA® Granular (45 mL)
1 tbsp red wine vinegar (15 mL)
1 tbsp white vinegar (15 mL)
1 tbsp lemon juice (15 mL)
$^1/_4$ tsp dry mustard (1 mL)
$^1/_4$ tsp salt, OR to taste (1 mL)

Yield: 1 cup (250 mL)
1 tbsp (15 mL) per serving
69.9 calories
0.4 g protein
7.3 g fat
1.2 g carbs

Peel avocadoes, pit and chop coarsely. Place avocadoes in blender, along with olive oil, SPLENDA® Granular, red wine vinegar, white vinegar, lemon juice, dry mustard and salt. Blend until well combined. Scoop into dipping bowl in center of pretty serving dish. Surround with low-carb vegetables for dipping.

Variation: **Mexican-style Dip:** Stir in medium-hot Salsa and a few bright green bits of avocado (soaked in lemon juice). The mixture will turn light brown in color, however, it is not an unpleasant color with the green avocado. Place some bright red Salsa on top, if desired. The taste is very Mexican. Lovely as a condiment in Cheese Tacos, page 33, *More Splendid Low-Carbing*. Also great for dipping chicken strips.

STRAWBERRY BANANA CREAM DIP

An incredible fruit dip. It keeps its consistency in the refrigerator and out.

4 oz regular cream cheese, (125 g)
  softened
$^1/_2$ cup plain yogurt (125 mL)
$^1/_2$ cup Crème Fraiche, page 54 (125 mL)
$^1/_2$ cup SPLENDA® Granular (125 mL)
1 tbsp Da Vinci® Sugar Free (15 mL)
  Banana Syrup
1 tbsp Da Vinci® Sugar Free (15 mL)
  Strawberry Syrup

Yield: $1^1/_2$ cups (375 mL)
1 tsp (5 mL) per serving
10.1 calories
0.3 g protein
0.8 g fat
0.3 g carbs

In food processor with sharp blade, or blender, process cream cheese until smooth. Add yogurt, Crème Fraiche, page 54, SPLENDA® Granular and Da Vinci® Sugar Free Banana and Strawberry Syrups; process until light and smooth. Serve with your favorite low-carb fruits.

SOUPS & SALADS

BACON 'N AVOCADO SALAD

The dressing for this salad is out of this world! This recipe is a gift from a dear friend, Jeanne Lobsinger of Vernon, British Columbia, Canada, who unofficially adopted me! She is a neat person, fabulous cook, businesswoman, gardener, artist and singer, to name but a few of her talents.

8 cups torn Romaine lettuce (2 L)
8 slices bacon, cooked crisp and
  crumbled
2 avocadoes, peeled, pitted and chopped
Dressing:
$^{1}/_{2}$ cup olive oil (125 mL)
$^{1}/_{2}$ cup chopped onion (125 mL)
$^{1}/_{3}$ cup SPLENDA® Granular (75 mL)
$^{1}/_{4}$ cup tomato paste (50 mL)
2 tbsp Worcestershire sauce (25 mL)
$^{1}/_{2}$ tsp dry mustard (2 mL)
$^{1}/_{2}$ tsp salt (2 mL)
$^{1}/_{2}$ tsp hot cayenne pepper (2 mL)

Yield: 8 servings
1 serving
267.1 calories
8.3 g protein
23.3 g fat
6.0 g carbs

In salad spinner, rinse Romaine lettuce well and spin dry. Add bacon and chopped avocado.

In blender, blend olive oil, chopped onion, SPLENDA® Granular, tomato paste, Worcestershire sauce, dry mustard, salt and hot cayenne pepper, until smooth and thick.

Pour dressing over salad and toss. Serve immediately.

Helpful Hint: The dressing makes a great sauce for dipping chicken or shrimp.

SESAME GINGER CHICKEN SALAD

A delicious salad; the dressing is special!

8 cups Romaine lettuce (2 L)
$^1/_2$ cup chopped fresh parsley, (125 mL)
  (optional)
4 cooked boneless chicken breast halves,
  cut into strips or cubed
10 oz can mandarin oranges, (284 mL)
  in juice, drained
1 cup peeled and julienned or (250 mL)
  chopped jicama, OR cucumber
2 tbsp sesame seeds, toasted (25 mL)

Sesame Ginger Dressing:
$^1/_2$ cup olive oil (125 mL)
3 tbsp white vinegar (45 mL)
2 tbsp peeled ginger root, (25 mL)
  minced
2 tbsp sesame seeds, toasted (25 mL)
2 tbsp chopped onion (25 mL)
1 tbsp SPLENDA® Granular (15 mL)
1 tbsp soy sauce (15 mL)
1 tsp tomato paste (5 mL)
$^1/_8$ tsp white pepper (0.5 mL)

Yield: 8 servings
1 serving
243.0 calories
15.6 g protein
16.7 g fat
7.0 g carbs

Place rinsed lettuce and parsley, if using, in salad bowl. Toss lettuce with chicken, mandarin orange segments and jicama or cucumber.

Sesame Ginger Dressing: In blender, combine olive oil, vinegar, ginger root, sesame seeds, onion, SPLENDA® Granular, soy sauce, tomato paste and pepper. Blend until smooth.

Pour dressing over salad, toss and sprinkle toasted sesame seeds over top.

Variation: Sesame Shrimp Salad: Substitute 20 oz (600 g) cooked salad shrimp. (*6.3 g Carbs*) If preferred, use 4 chopped, hard-boiled eggs, instead of mandarin oranges for a more savory salad. (*3.8 g Carbs*)

FRUIT SALAD

Yes, we can still enjoy fruit salad! I used a combination of fruit that is usually always available during the summer months, however, you can use your imagination and make other fruit salad combinations with other berries, etc.

2 cups strawberries, sliced (500 mL)
1 cup cantaloupe balls (250 mL)
2 kiwifruit, sliced and cut in half

Yield: 6 servings
1 serving
45.0 calories
0.9 g protein
0.4 g fat
8.4 g carbs

In pretty fruit salad bowl, combine strawberries, cantaloupe balls and kiwifruit. Serve with a dollop Crème Fraiche, page 54, or Any-Flavor Syrup, page 52, if desired.

Helpful Hint: It has been determined that our insulin sensitivity is more acute in the mornings, therefore, occasionally, happily indulge in this lovely summer fruit salad instead of eggs and bacon for breakfast.

EXOTIC AVOCADO MOLD

Don't tell anyone there's avocado in this salad, and they'll never guess! Avocado pears are actually a fruit.

1 1/2 envelopes unflavored gelatin
1/2 cup SPLENDA® Granular (125 mL)
1 envelope sugar free Lemon Kool-Aid®
1 tbsp lime juice (15 mL)
1 cup boiling water (250 mL)
1/2 cup mayonnaise (125 mL)
1 avocado, mashed
1/4 cup chopped pecans (50 mL)
1/8 tsp garlic powder (0.5 mL)
1/8 tsp onion salt (0.5 mL)
4 oz light cream cheese, diced (125 g)

Yield: 8 servings
1 serving
204.5 calories
3.1 g protein
19.9 g fat
3.5 g carbs

In medium bowl, combine gelatin, SPLENDA® Granular, Lemon Kool-Aid,® and lime juice. Whisk in boiling water until gelatin dissolves. Stir in mayonnaise, avocado, pecans, garlic powder and onion salt. Add cream cheese. Pour into 4-cup (1 L) mold. Cover and refrigerate until set.

LOW-CARBER'S SPECIAL

Plenty of protein in this delightful salad, with a particularly tasty dressing.

4 cups torn Romaine lettuce (1 L)
1 cup sliced fresh mushrooms (250 mL)
$^1/_4$ cup chopped green onions (50 mL)
4 slices bacon, cooked crisp,
  and crumbled
2 hard-boiled eggs, sliced

Dressing:
$^1/_4$ cup light-tasting olive oil (50 mL)
2 tbsp SPLENDA® Granular (25 mL)
2 tbsp tomato paste (25 mL)
1 tbsp white vinegar (15 mL)
$1^1/_2$ tsp Worcestershire sauce (7 mL)
$^1/_4$ tsp onion salt (1 mL)
$^1/_8$ tsp garlic powder (0.5 mL)

Yield: 4 servings
1 serving
227.2 calories
10.7 g protein
18.2 g fat
4.3 g carbs

In large salad bowl, combine rinsed Romaine lettuce, mushrooms, green onions, bacon and hard-boiled eggs.

Dressing: In blender, blend olive oil, SPLENDA® Granular, tomato paste, white vinegar, Worcestershire sauce, onion salt and garlic powder. Toss salad with dressing just before serving.

Variation: Omit mushrooms and use one avocado, peeled and sliced instead. (**5.4 g Carbs**)

MEXICAN CHICKEN SOUP

Adding avocado and grated cheese is what makes this soup really special.

1 tbsp olive oil (15 mL)
$^1/_2$ cup chopped onion (125 mL)
5 cups water (1.25 L)
2 tsp ground cumin (10 mL)
$^3/_4$ tsp hot chili powder (3 mL)
$^1/_2$ tsp salt (2 mL)
$^1/_2$ tsp black pepper (2 mL)
$^1/_2$ tsp garlic powder (2 mL)
$^1/_8$ tsp Thickening Agent, page 57 (0.5 mL)
1$^1/_4$ lbs cooked chicken, (0.567 kg)
  cut into bite size pieces
1 cup diced tomatoes (250 mL)
1$^1/_2$ avocadoes, peeled, pitted and diced
$^1/_2$ cup grated Cheddar cheese (125 mL)

> **Yield:** 6 servings
> 1 servings
> 258.5 calories
> 25.9 g protein
> 14.6 g fat
> **4.8 g carbs**

In large saucepan, heat oil and add chopped onion, cooking until soft. Stir in water, cumin, hot chili powder, salt, black pepper, garlic powder and Thickening Agent, page 57. Bring to boil and simmer 20 minutes. Add chicken and tomatoes. Simmer 5 more minutes. Serve topped with avocado and grated Cheddar cheese.

JEANNE'S SQUASH SOUP

Jeanne Lobsinger is a sweet lady who often makes delicious, nutritious soups.

1 cup chopped onion (250 mL)
2 tbsp butter (25 mL)
2 medium Butternut squash, peeled
  and coarsely chopped
5 cups chicken broth (1.25 L)
1 tsp thyme (5 mL)
$^1/_2$ cup plain yogurt (125 mL)
$^1/_2$ tsp salt, or to taste (2 mL)
$^1/_2$ tsp black pepper, or to taste (2 mL)

> **Yield:** 7 cups (1.75 L)
> 1 cup (250 mL) per serving
> 77.7 calories
> 1.7 g protein
> 4.0 g fat
> **7.9 g carbs**

In large saucepan, over medium heat, sauté onions in butter until translucent. Add squash and cook 5 minutes. Add broth and thyme. Cook 25 minutes over medium heat, or until squash is soft. Set aside 1 cup (250 mL) of soup. In blender, puree remainder of soup. Return pureed mixture to saucepan along with reserved soup. Add yogurt, salt and pepper and heat almost to boiling.

FAUX BAKED POTATO SOUP

Terrific soup with some of the topping ingredients of a baked potato.

1 head of cauliflower, about
  medium size, chopped small
1 tbsp olive oil (15 mL)
2 tbsp finely chopped onion (25 mL)
4 cups water (1 L)
4 tsp instant chicken stock mix (20 mL)
3 oz grated Cheddar cheese (90 g)
$^1/_4$ cup whipping cream (50 mL)
$^1/_4$ cup water (50 mL)
4 slices bacon, cooked crisp and chopped
3 tbsp fresh chopped chives (45 mL)
1 tsp ground black pepper (5 mL)
1 tbsp butter (15 mL)
salt to taste

Yield: 6 servings
1 serving
183.8 calories
9.9 g protein
13.6 g fat
5.1 g carbs

Steam cauliflower until just tender, about 25 minutes. Drain. In deep nonstick saucepan, in oil, fry onion until tender. Add cauliflower, water and instant chicken stock mix. Bring to boil.

Puree half soup in blender. Return to saucepan. Add cheese, whipping cream, water, bacon, chives and black pepper. Heat until cheese has melted. Stir in butter. Add salt to taste and serve.

Add a dollop of sour cream on top, if desired.

Helpful Hint: 4 Cups (1 L) chicken broth may be used instead of water and instant chicken stock mix.

GARDEN CREAM OF TOMATO SOUP

Use fresh tomatoes out of your garden, if you have them. Low sodium soup for salt-conscious folks.

$^1/_4$ cup chopped onion (50 mL)
2 tbsp butter (25 mL)
4 large ripe tomatoes, coarsely
  chopped, OR 6 plum tomatoes, chopped
$^3/_4$ cup water (175 mL)
$^1/_4$ cup whipping cream (50 mL)
$^1/_4$ cup sour cream (50 mL)
1 tsp thyme (5 mL)
1 tsp SPLENDA® Granular (5 mL)
$^1/_2$ tsp black pepper (2 mL)
$^1/_2$ tsp onion salt (2 mL)

Yield: 4 generous servings
1 serving
149.1 calories
2.0 g protein
13.0 g fat
6.3 g carbs

In large skillet, stir-fry onion in butter until softened. Add tomatoes and cook until softened; about 10 minutes. Allow tomato mixture to cool slightly and blend well in blender. If desired, strain.

In medium saucepan, pour tomato soup. Add water, whipping cream, sour cream, thyme, SPLENDA® Granular, black pepper and onion salt. Heat soup to scalding.

Serve with grated Cheddar cheese or a dollop of sour cream.

Helpful Hints: Add extra salt to taste, if desired. For those who don't care for thyme, substitute $^1/_2$ tsp (2 mL) hot pepper sauce instead, or to taste.

BREAKFAST

CREAM CHEESE BRAN WAFFLES

These waffles are great with strawberries or strawberry fruit spread and whipped topping. Use in place of bread, if desired, for breakfast.

16 oz regular cream cheese, (500 g)
  softened
6 eggs
1 cup Whey Ultimate Bake Mix, (250 mL)
  page 67
1 cup wheat bran (250 mL)
$^1/_4$ cup half-and-half cream (50 mL)
$^1/_4$ cup water (50 mL)
2 tbsp SPLENDA® Granular (25 mL)
1 tsp baking soda (5 mL)
1 tsp baking powder (5 mL)
$^1/_4$ tsp salt (1 mL)

> *Yield:* 22 waffles
> 1 waffle
> 122.1 calories
> 6.1 g protein
> 9.2 g fat
> *3.2 g carbs*

In food processor with sharp blade, or in bowl with electric mixer, process cream cheese until smooth. Add eggs; process. Add Whey Ultimate Bake Mix, page 67, wheat bran, half-and-half cream, water, SPLENDA® Granular, baking soda, baking powder and salt. Process.

Pour by $^1/_4$ cup (50 mL) onto hot, greased waffle iron. Close and cook according to manufacturer's instructions. Toast in toaster afterwards for crisper results.

Variation: **Savory Cheese Waffles:** Omit wheat bran, SPLENDA® Granular and salt. Add $2^1/_2$ cups (625 mL) Cheddar cheese, $^1/_2$ tsp (2 mL) garlic powder and $^1/_4$ tsp (1 mL) onion salt. *Yield:* 22 waffles. (*2.7 g Carbs*)

Helpful Hint: See Nutella® -like topping for waffles, page 94.

ULTRA LOW-CARB PANCAKES

These involve no guilt. I enjoy them with strawberries and Crème Fraiche, page 54, or just plain, buttered, or with Flavored Sweet Butters, page 59. The Flap Jacks (no flour) serve well as little sandwiches for various fillings.

2 extra-large eggs
$^{1}/_{4}$ cup Ricotta, OR Cottage (50 mL)
  cheese
2 tbsp vanilla whey protein (25 mL)
2 tbsp vital wheat gluten (25 mL)
1 tsp baking powder (5 mL)
$^{1}/_{8}$ tsp salt, optional (0.5 mL)
$1^{1}/_{2}$ tsp olive oil (7 mL)

Yield: 10 pancakes
1 Ricotta/Cottage pancake
36.8/34.9 calories
3.7/3.8 g protein
2.1/1.8 g fat
0.8/0.8 g carbs

In medium bowl, beat eggs with fork until frothy. Stir in Ricotta cheese or Cottage cheese, vanilla whey protein, vital wheat gluten, baking powder and salt, if using.

In large nonstick electric frying pan or skillet, spread half olive oil around. Drop 5 rounded tablespoonfuls of batter onto hot skillet. Cook until bubbles form. Turn over and cook briefly on other side. Stir batter and repeat.

Variations: **Flap Jacks (no flour):** Double main recipe above and stir in an extra $^{1}/_{4}$ cup (50 mL) Ricotta or Cottage cheese, 1 tsp (5 mL) vanilla extract and 1 tbsp (15 mL) SPLENDA® Granular. Omit baking powder and vital wheat gluten. Use $^{1}/_{2}$ cup (125 mL) vanilla whey protein and $^{1}/_{8}$ tsp salt (optional).

Drop by 4 teaspoonfuls (measuring spoons come in this size too) onto hot, greased skillet. ***Yield:*** 23 Flap Jacks. 1 Flap Jack: (***0.5 g Carbs***)

Cream Cheese Flap Jacks: Double main recipe above, substituting 4 oz (125 g) regular cream cheese total for Ricotta cheese. Use 1 tsp (5 mL) baking powder. Omit salt. Drop by 4 teaspoonfuls onto hot, greased skillet. When Flap Jacks form bubbles, flip and cook other side.
Yield: 23 Cream Cheese Flap Jacks. 1 Flap Jack. (***0.6 g Carbs***)

Helpful Hints: With savory fillings, use natural whey protein powder without sucralose. My favorite way to eat these Flap Jack "sandwiches" is spread with Cinnamon Butter, page 59, and topped with a slice of Mozzarella cheese and another Flap Jack. Nuke approximately 12 seconds. These pancakes are a little flat, but taste good. The Cream Cheese Flap Jacks are slightly thicker.

CRUNCHY GRANOLA

Excellent sprinkled over plain yogurt, which has been flavored and sweetened with Da Vinci® Sugar Free Syrup.

2 cups medium-flaked coconut (500 mL)
1¹/₂ cups vanilla whey protein (375 mL)
1¹/₄ cups diced almonds (300 mL)
¹/₂ cup SPLENDA® Granular (125 mL)
¹/₂ cup wheat germ, OR flax (125 mL)
  seed meal
¹/₂ cup quick-cooking oats (125 mL)
3 rye crisp bread crackers, broken into
  small pieces
1 tsp cinnamon (5 mL)
¹/₃ cup butter, melted (75 mL)
¹/₃ cup coconut oil, melted (75 mL)
¹/₃ cup Da Vinci® Sugar Free Cinnamon Syrup (75 mL)

> **Yield:** 6¹/₂ cups (1.625 L)
> ¹/₄ cup (50 mL) per serving
> 180.1 calories
> 6.2 g protein
> 14.3 g fat
> *5.2 g carbs*

In large bowl, combine coconut, vanilla whey protein, almonds, SPLENDA® Granular, wheat germ or flax seed meal, oats, rye crisp bread pieces (small pieces) and cinnamon.

Stir in butter, coconut oil and Da Vinci® Sugar Free Cinnamon Syrup, until well combined.

Spread granola out on 2 greased cookie sheets (spray with nonstick cooking spray) and bake in 300°F (150°C) oven 25 to 30 minutes, or until turning golden brown. Stir granola once during cooking time.

Variation: **Da Vinci® Alternative:** Use water, 2 tbsp (25 mL) SPLENDA® Granular and ¹/₂ tsp (2 mL) extra cinnamon.

BREAKFAST PIZZA

Guilt-free pizza for breakfast! This is quite pleasant indeed.

Pizza Crust:
4 eggs
$^1/_2$ cup Ricotta cheese, OR (125 mL)
   Cottage cheese
$^1/_2$ cup Mozzarella, OR (125 mL)
   Cheddar cheese
$^1/_4$ cup vanilla whey protein (50 mL)
$^1/_4$ cup vital wheat gluten (50 mL)
2 tsp baking powder (10 mL)

Pizza Sauce:
3 tbsp tomato sauce (45 mL)
2 tbsp tomato paste (25 mL)
1 tsp SPLENDA® Granular (5 mL)
$^1/_2$ tsp basil (2 mL)

Toppings:
8 thin slices ham, OR other deli meat
$1^1/_2$ cups Mozzarella cheese (375 mL)

Yield: 12 servings
1 serving
153.0 calories
15.3 g protein
8.7 g fat
2.8 g carbs

Pizza Crust: In large bowl, beat eggs with fork until frothy. Stir in Ricotta or Cottage cheese, Mozzarella or Cheddar cheese, vanilla whey protein, vital wheat gluten and baking powder.

Pour into greased pizza pan. Bake in 325°F (160°C) oven 15 minutes.

Pizza Sauce: In small bowl, combine tomato sauce, tomato paste, SPLENDA® Granular and basil. Spread over baked pizza crust. Top with ham and Mozzarella cheese.

Bake in 350°F (180°C) oven 15 minutes, or until cheese has melted. Place 10-inches (25 cm) from broiler and broil approximately 2 to 3 minutes. Set timer and watch carefully.

ROAST BEEF ROLL-UPS

This is one of my favorite meals for breakfast. It keeps me going for hours.

1.5 oz roast beef, sliced thinly, (45 g)
  Deli-style (about 5 slices)
$2^1/_2$ tsp Horseradish Cream (12 mL)
  Sauce, page 55
5 canned asparagus spears
$^1/_3$ cup grated Mozzarella cheese (75 mL)

Yield: 1 serving
1 serving
341.3 calories
24.0 g protein
26.0 g fat
1.8 g carbs

Spread roast beef with $^1/_2$ tsp (2 mL) Horseradish Cream Sauce, page 55. Place one asparagus spear in center. Sprinkle with 1 tbsp (15 mL) cheese. Roll up. Microwave 10 seconds and enjoy! Or, simply roll up and eat cold.

OAT DROP BISCUITS

Lovely, flaky biscuits for a change of pace in the morning.

2 cups Vital Oat Ultimate Bake (500 mL)
  Mix, page 67
4 tsp baking powder (20 mL)
1 tsp SPLENDA® Granular (5 mL)
$^1/_2$ tsp cream of tartar (5 mL)
$^1/_2$ cup butter (125 mL)
1 cup grated Cheddar cheese, (250 mL)
  (optional)
1 extra-large egg
$^1/_3$ cup whipping cream (75 mL)
$^1/_4$ cup olive oil (50 mL)
$^1/_4$ cup water (50 mL)

Yield: 12 biscuits
1 biscuit
226.1 calories
6.1 g protein
20.2 g fat
4.7 g carbs

In large bowl, combine Vital Oat Ultimate Bake Mix, page 67, baking powder, SPLENDA® Granular and cream of tartar. Rub in butter. Stir in Cheddar cheese. In another bowl, beat egg with fork. Stir in cream, olive oil and water. Add liquid ingredients to Vital Oat Ultimate Bake Mixture.

Drop batter onto a greased baking sheet by about $2^1/_2$ tablespoonfuls (32 mL). Bake in 450°F (230°C) oven 8 to 10 minutes, or until turning brown in spots.

Helpful Hint: One biscuit with Cheddar cheese in it: (***4.8 g Carbs***). These are higher in calories, so the above recipe is preferable if calories are a concern.

FAUX BLUEBERRY OATMEAL

Served warm with low-carb syrup, this breakfast reminds me a bit of oatmeal with blueberries in it. Try it and see if you agree!

1 $^1/_2$ cups cottage cheese (375 mL)
4 eggs, fork beaten
$^1/_2$ cup Nut-Free Oat UBM (125 mL)
  Mix, page 68
$^1/_4$ cup SPLENDA® Granular (50 mL)
2 tbsp butter, melted (25 mL)
2 tsp vanilla extract (10 mL)
1 cup frozen blueberries (250 mL)

> *Yield:* 6 large servings
> 1 serving
> 180.2 calories
> 15.0 g protein
> 8.8 g fat
> *7.6 g carbs*

In large bowl, combine cottage cheese, eggs, Nut-Free Oat Ultimate Bake Mix, page 68, SPLENDA® Granular, butter and vanilla extract. Stir in blueberries. Pour into greased 9 x 13-inch (23 x 33 cm) glass baking dish and bake in 350°F (180°C) oven 30 minutes, or until set. Allow to cool slightly.

CALIFORNIA OMELET

I can imagine a sunny California day as I enjoy this omelet – one of my favorites!

1 extra-large egg
1 tsp water (5 mL)
$^1/_8$ tsp Tabasco sauce (0.5 mL)
dash salt and pepper
1.5 oz salad shrimp, thawed (45 g)
0.5 oz grated Cheddar cheese (15 g)
$^1/_4$ California avocado, chopped

> *Yield:* 1 omelet
> 1 serving
> 253.2 calories
> 19.3 g protein
> 17.9 g fat
> *3.0 g carbs*

In cereal bowl, combine egg, water, Tabasco sauce, salt and pepper. Beat with fork. Pour into nonstick 6-inch (15 cm) omelet pan. Cook over medium heat until beginning to set. Arrange shrimp and cheddar cheese on one side. Cook until set. Flip other side over filling. Cook another minute, or until shrimp is heated and cheese has melted.

Sprinkle chopped avocado over omelet and a little extra grated cheese, if desired. Serve immediately.

MEAT

CROCK-POT BEEF ROAST

The gravy for this roast is so rich and flavorful. No need to first brown this roast, as it turns a lovely, rich brown color anyway.

2.2 lb beef roast, sirloin, OR (1 kg)
   rolled rump
Gravy:
$^1/_4$ cup tomato paste (50 mL)
$^1/_4$ cup tomato sauce (50 mL)
1 tbsp white vinegar (15 mL)
1 tbsp Worcestershire sauce (15 mL)
1 tbsp molasses (15 mL)
1 tbsp SPLENDA® Granular (15 mL)
1 tsp crushed garlic (5 mL)
$^1/_2$ tsp dry mustard (2 mL)
$^1/_2$ tsp hot chili powder (2 mL)
$1^1/_2$ tsp Thickening Agent, page 57 (7 mL)

Yield: 6 servings
1 serving
339.6 calories
36.0 g protein
18.2 g fat
5.5 g carbs

Place roast in crock-pot.

In medium bowl, combine tomato paste, tomato sauce, white vinegar, Worcestershire sauce, molasses, SPLENDA® Granular, garlic, dry mustard and hot chili powder. Pour over roast.

Cook on high one hour. Cook on low another 6 hours, or until meat thermometer registers 160°F (71°C) for medium or 170°F (77°C) for well done.

Remove roast. Stir Thickening Agent, page 57, into hot gravy, until thickened.

SWEET MUSTARD BAKED HAM

Easy instructions for baked ham.

2.2 lb fully cooked ham (1 kg)
4 whole cloves
Sweet Mustard Glaze:
$^1/_2$ cup SPLENDA® Granular (125 mL)
1 tbsp prepared mustard (15 mL)
$1^1/_2$ tsp Worcestershire sauce (7 mL)
$^1/_4$ tsp salt (1 mL)
$^1/_8$ tsp black pepper (0.5 mL)

Yield: 4 servings	
1 serving	
343.1 calories	
48.6 g protein	
12.5 g fat	
5.8 g carbs	

Sweet Mustard Glaze: In small bowl, combine SPLENDA® Granular, mustard, Worcestershire sauce, salt and black pepper.

Place ham on rack in shallow roasting pan. Score surface lightly and insert cloves.

Using pastry brush, brush surface of ham with Sweet Mustard Glaze and bake in 325°F (160°C) oven 1 hour and 30 minutes, or until meat thermometer registers 150°F (66°C).

Let stand 5 minutes. Slice thinly and serve with Creamy Mustard Sauce, page 60, *More Splendid Low-Carbing*, if desired.

Helpful Hints: To cut carbs a little, one could use $^1/_4$ cup (50 mL) Da Vinci® Sugar Free Pancake Syrup instead of SPLENDA® Granular, an extra tablespoon (15 mL) mustard and omit Worcestershire sauce. (**2.8 g Carbs**)

GREEK-STYLE LAMB

Tender lamb in rich gravy, sprinkled with fresh parsley and feta cheese.

2.2 lbs lamb shoulder, (1 kg)
  boneless
$^1/_4$ tsp salt (1 mL)
$^1/_4$ tsp black pepper (1 mL)
1 cup chopped onion (250 mL)
1 green pepper, chopped
1 cup tomato sauce (250 mL)
1 clove garlic, minced
2 tsp SPLENDA® Granular (10 mL)
1 tsp oregano (5 mL)
$^3/_4$ tsp salt (3 mL)
$^1/_2$ tsp instant chicken stock mix (2 mL)
$^1/_4$ tsp cinnamon (1 mL)
$^1/_4$ tsp rosemary (1 mL)
1 tsp Thickening Agent, page 57 (5 mL)
$^2/_3$ cup crumbled feta cheese (150 mL)
$^1/_4$ cup chopped fresh parsley (50 mL)

Yield: 6 servings
1 serving
278.2 calories
36.0 g protein
10.8 g fat
6.7 g carbs

Sprinkle lamb with salt and pepper. Place in crock-pot. In medium bowl, combine onion, green pepper, tomato sauce, garlic, SPLENDA® Granular, oregano, salt, instant chicken stock mix, cinnamon and rosemary. Pour over lamb.

On low heat, cook 7 hours or until lamb registers 180°F (82°C) on meat thermometer. (This will mean the lamb is well done; 175°F (79°C) would mean medium).

About one or two hours before end of cooking time, sprinkle in Thickening Agent, page 57, and stir well. Cover and continue to cook. Remove lamb to casserole dish. Pour gravy overall. Garnish with feta cheese and fresh parsley.

PORK VINDALOO

Fabulously spicy, tender pork dish.

2 tbsp fruit chutney*, (25 mL)
  sugar free, preferably
2-inch piece fresh ginger, peeled and
  minced
2 tbsp cider vinegar (25 mL)
2 tbsp water (25 mL)
1 tbsp crushed garlic (15 mL)
2 tsp ground cumin (10 mL)
2 tsp black pepper (10 mL)
2 tsp poppy seeds (10 mL)
2 tsp SPLENDA® Granular (10 mL)
1½ tsp hot cayenne pepper (7 mL)
1 tsp dried chilies (5 mL)
1 tsp salt (5 mL)
1 tsp Thickening Agent, page 57 (5 mL)
½ tsp ground cloves (2 mL)
¼ tsp ground anise star (1 mL)
1 onion, finely chopped
1 green pepper, finely chopped
1 yellow, orange or red pepper, finely chopped
¼ cup olive oil (50 mL)
4 lbs pork tenderloin boneless chops, (1.9 kg)
  cut into small bite-size pieces
¾ cup water (175 mL)

Yield: 10 servings
1 serving
411.7 calories
38 g protein
25.6 g fat
5.1 g carbs

In small bowl, combine chutney, ginger, cider vinegar, water, garlic, cumin, black pepper, poppy seeds, SPLENDA® Granular, hot cayenne pepper, dried chilies, salt, Thickening Agent, page 57, ground cloves and anise star. Set aside.

In large electric frying pan, in 2 tbsp (25 mL) olive oil, fry onion, green and yellow, orange or red pepper until tender. Add spice mixture and cook 5 minutes, while stirring.

Add remaining oil and pork; cook 5 minutes, turning often to distribute spices. Place pork and vegetables in crock-pot. Add water, cover and cook over low heat 7 to 8 hours. Serve over Cauli-Fried Rice, page 53, *More Splendid Low-Carbing*.

MOZZARELLA BEEF ROLL

This meat loaf is a little more fancy than the usual.

$1^1/_2$ lbs lean ground beef (0.680 kg)
$^1/_3$ cup wheat bran (75 mL)
1 egg
1 tbsp dehydrated minced onion (15 mL)
1 tsp salt (5 mL)
$^1/_4$ tsp black pepper (1 mL)
$1^1/_2$ cups Mozzarella cheese (375 mL)
Sauce:
1 cup tomato sauce (250 mL)
1 tbsp Worcestershire sauce (15 mL)
1 tbsp SPLENDA® Granular (15 mL)
10 oz can sliced mushroom (284 mL)

Yield: 10 servings	
1 serving	
297.1 calories	
22.9 g protein	
20.5 g fat	
3.8 g carbs	

In large bowl, place ground beef and wheat bran. In small bowl, beat egg with fork and stir in onion, salt and pepper. Add to ground beef mixture and mix until well combined.

Lay wax paper out on cookie sheet. Press out ground beef into large rectangle, almost the size of cookie sheet. Sprinkle cheese over top, and approximately $^3/_4$-inch (2 cm) from edges. Roll up, using wax paper to help, however, remove wax paper. Place seam side down in 9 x 13-inch (23 x 33 cm) glass baking dish.

Sauce: In small bowl, combine tomato sauce, Worcestershire sauce and SPLENDA® Granular.

Spread half sauce over beef roll and bake in 375°F (190°C) oven 45 minutes. Stir mushrooms into remaining tomato sauce and spread over roll. Bake 15 minutes longer.

SIRLOIN STEAK IN BUTTER SAUCE

Ooooh, so good!!! Peppery steak, chock full of flavor.

4 lbs sirloin steak, about (1.8 kg)
 1$^1/_2$ inches (3.8 cm) thick
Butter Sauce:
1 cup butter (250 mL)
3 tbsp Worcestershire sauce (45 mL)
2 tbsp dehydrated onion (25 mL)
2 tbsp dried parsley (25 mL)
2 tsp ground black pepper (10 mL)
1 tsp dry mustard (5 mL)
1 tsp salt, OR to taste (5 mL)

Yield: 10 servings
1 serving
428.8 calories
41.3 g protein
28.0 g fat
1.3 g carbs

Lightly score edges of steak at 1-inch intervals.

Butter Sauce: In small saucepan, heat butter, Worcestershire sauce, dehydrated onion, parsley, black pepper, mustard and salt to boiling. Turn heat low and simmer 10 minutes, or until onion is soft.

Keep aside some Butter Sauce in gravy boat for serving at the table.

Place steak on barbecue grill and brush with butter sauce. Baste steak and cook 6 minutes, turn and baste again, cooking another 6 minutes, or until medium done.

Cut steak into slices across the grain and drizzle reserved butter sauce over steak.

ZUCCHINI LASAGNA

A nice way to eat this vegetable as a main course.

1 lb lean ground beef (0.454 kg)
1 cup tomato sauce (250 mL)
2 tsp basil (10 mL)
1 tsp salt (5 mL)
$^1/_2$ tsp black pepper (2 mL)
$2^1/_2$ lbs zucchini (1.1 kg)
2 tbsp spelt or soy flour, divided (25 mL)
1 cup Ricotta cheese (250 mL)
1 egg, fork beaten
2 tbsp spelt or soy flour, divided (25 mL)
$1^1/_2$ cups grated Mozzarella cheese (375 mL)
2 tbsp grated Parmesan cheese (25 mL)

Yield: 12 servings
1 serving
211.3 calories
18.6 g protein
12.5 g fat
4.3 g carbs

In large skillet, brown beef; pour off excess fat. Stir in tomato sauce, basil, salt and black pepper.

Slice zucchini lengthwise into $^1/_4$–inch (0.6 cm) thick slices.

In small bowl, combine Ricotta cheese and egg.

Arrange half zucchini in bottom of 13 x 9-inch (4 L) pan and sprinkle with half spelt or soy flour. Top with half Ricotta cheese mixture, half meat sauce and other half Ricotta cheese mixture. Repeat zucchini, remaining flour, and meat sauce layers.

Top with Mozzarella and Parmesan cheeses. Bake in 375°F (190°C) oven 40 minutes.

FRUITED PORK

Delicious! Try the variation as well.

4 lbs pork loin tenderloin (1.9 kg)
  boneless chops
$1/4$ cup olive oil (50 mL)
$1^1/2$ cups orange juice (375 mL)
$1/3$ cup SPLENDA® Granular (75 mL)
$1/4$ cup Da Vinci® Sugar Free (50 mL)
  Orange Syrup
$1/4$ cup lemon juice (50 mL)
2 tbsp Worcestershire sauce (25 mL)
2 tsp salt (10 mL)
$1/2$ tsp black pepper (2 mL)
1 tbsp Thickening Agent, page 57 (15 mL)
1 cup canned mandarin oranges (250 mL)
$1/4$ cup raisins, snipped (50 mL)

Yield: 12 servings.
1 serving
275.1 calories
38.5 g protein
8.5 g fat
9.0 g carbs

In large electric frying pan, brown meat in olive oil. Transfer to crock-pot.

In saucepan, combine orange juice, SPLENDA® Granular, Da Vinci® Sugar Free Orange Syrup, lemon juice, Worcestershire sauce, salt and black pepper. Bring to boil. Sprinkle with Thickening Agent, page 57, and whisk. Stir in mandarin oranges and raisins. Pour over pork chops.

Cook on low 8 hours.

Variation: **Curried Fruited Pork:** Add 1 tsp (5 mL) hot curry powder, page 61, *More Splendid Low-Carbing*.

Da Vinci® Alternative: Use 1 tsp (5 mL) orange extract, water and increase SPLENDA® Granular to $1/2$ cup (125 mL). (*9.4 g Carbs*)

POULTRY

TERIYAKI CHICKEN

Super marinade! Great for chicken drumettes too.

3.5 lbs chicken breasts, (1.6 kg)
  bone-in
Teriyaki Marinade:
6 tbsp soy sauce (90 mL)
6 tbsp SPLENDA® Granular (90 mL)
2 tbsp water (25 mL)
2 tsp ground ginger (10 mL)
1 tsp garlic powder (5 mL)
$^1/_2$ tsp Thickening Agent, page 57 (2 mL)

Yield: 6 servings
1 serving
227.5 calories
32.2 g protein
8.5 g fat
3.4 g carbs

Wash chicken breasts and pat dry with paper towels. Place chicken in 9 x 13-inch (23 x 33 cm) glass baking dish.

Teriyaki Marinade: In small bowl, combine soy sauce, SPLENDA® Granular, water, ground ginger, garlic powder and Thickening Agent, page 57.

Pour Teriyaki Marinade over chicken. Marinate 2 hours in refrigerator.

Bake in 350°F (180°C) oven 1 hour. Halfway through baking, baste chicken with marinade.

ROAST CHICKEN

This roast chicken is rubbed with a tasty spice mixture. Nutritional analysis shown is without stuffing; as everyone will eat varying amounts, however, on average, add 5.0 g carbs.

5 lb roasting chicken (2.2 kg)
Bread-Sausage Stuffing, page 55
Spice Rub:
2 tsp paprika (10 mL)
$1^1/_2$ tsp salt (7 mL)
1 tsp thyme (5 mL)
$^1/_2$ tsp onion salt (2 mL)
$^1/_2$ tsp garlic powder (2 mL)
$^1/_2$ tsp black pepper (2 mL)
$^1/_4$ tsp hot cayenne pepper (1 mL)

Yield: 4 servings
1 serving
364.0 calories
41.1 g protein
20.6 g fat
1.0 g carbs

Rinse chicken and pat dry with paper towels. Stuff with Bread-Sausage Stuffing, page 55.

Spice Rub: In small bowl, combine paprika, salt, thyme, onion salt, garlic powder, black pepper and hot cayenne pepper. Stir well.

Rub chicken all over with Spice Rub. Place chicken, breast side up, in large roasting pan. Roast uncovered in 325°F (160°C) oven 2 to $2^1/_2$ hours, or until meat thermometer registers 180°F (82°C).

Helpful Hints: Surround chicken with sliced yams and small roasting potatoes and onions, if desired, for low-carbers on maintenance or non low-carbers.

For low-carbers, add sliced eggplant, mushrooms, halved tomatoes and thickly sliced zucchini, for instance, in the last hour of cooking. Baste vegetables with olive oil and sprinkle with paprika. Baste halfway through roasting with juices in roasting pan, turning vegetables.

For a breadless stuffing, see Sausage Apple Stuffing, page 62, of *Splendid Low-Carbing.*

CHICKEN FAJITA IN A TACO

Use in a low-carb tortilla, if desired (see below).

2 slices bacon
1 tsp olive oil (5 mL)
2 tbsp chopped onion (25 mL)
2 tbsp chopped green pepper (25 mL)
2.4 oz Cheddar cheese (68 g)
$^2/_3$ cup thin slivers of chicken, (150 mL)
  (cooked) - warmed
2 tbsp shredded lettuce (25 mL)
2 tbsp Salsa (25 mL)
2 tbsp sour cream (25 mL)

Yield: 2 servings
1 serving
277.4 calories
28.8 g protein
16.0 g fat
3.5 g carbs

Cook bacon on microwave bacon rack (covered with paper towel) until crisp or cook on dinner plate in microwave oven, using paper towels; chop finely and set aside. In small skillet in 1 tsp (5 mL) olive oil, cook onion and green pepper until tender. Keep warm.

Cheese Taco Shell: Spread 1.2 oz (34 g) grated Cheddar cheese to cover surface in nonstick 6-inch (15 cm) pan. Melt until turning brown and it begins to bubble up, or until it flips easily (takes a while); flip, cook very briefly and fold over.

Fill warm taco with half the warm chicken, bacon, onion, green pepper, lettuce, Salsa and sour cream. Repeat with next taco. Serve immediately.

Variation: **Chicken Wrap:** Use a 6-inch (15 cm) low-carb tortilla (two featured in *Splendid Low-Carbing*) instead of the cheese taco shell.
Subtract: (136.9 calories, 8.5 g protein, 11.3 g fat, *0.4 g carbs*) from the above nutritional analysis and add the analysis for your low-carb tortilla.

Helpful Hint: If taco becomes too brittle to fill without breaking, warm in microwave oven 25 to 30 seconds and fill.

CHUNKY TURKEY CHILI

A whole meal in a bowl.

1 tbsp olive oil (15 mL)
1 green pepper, cut into short,
  thin strips
1 lb leftover cooked turkey, (0.454 kg)
  coarsely chopped
1³/₄ cups tomato sauce (425 mL)
1¹/₄ cups water (300 mL)
2 tsp chili powder (10 mL)
2 tsp ground cumin (10 mL)
¹/₂ tsp crushed red pepper (2 mL)
1 cup grated Cheddar cheese (250 mL)
Optional Toppings:
Sour cream
chopped fresh cilantro
chopped avocado
chopped chives or green onions

Yield: 4 servings
1 serving
339.6 calories
34.2 g protein
17.6 g fat
9.4 g carbs

In large saucepan, in hot oil, stir fry green pepper until tender.

Add turkey, tomato sauce, water, chili powder, ground cumin and crushed red pepper. Bring to boil. Stir in ¹/₂ cup (125 mL) Cheddar cheese, until melted.

Sprinkle remaining cheese over each serving. Serve with one or more of the optional toppings, if desired.

Helpful Hint: Leftover cooked chicken may be used instead.

CHICKEN ALFREDO IN CREPES

Ian thought these were great! It sure doesn't seem like a low-carb meal.

Barbo's Crepes, page 71
Alfredo Sauce, page 93,
  Splendid Low-Carbing, OR use
  commercial bottled Alfredo Sauce
4 cups cooked chicken, (1 L)
  coarsely chopped
2 avocadoes, peeled and sliced

Yield: 12 crepes
1 crepe
338.9 calories
35.0 g protein
20.1 g fat
2.9 g carbs

Barbo's Crepes: Prepare Barbo's Crepes, page 71. Keep warm in low oven.

Alfredo Sauce: Prepare Alfredo Sauce, page 93, *Splendid Low-Carbing.* Add chicken to sauce.

Place small amount of filling on each crepe, add an avocado slice or two; roll up burrito-style. Serve immediately with a little salsa, if desired.

OVEN BAKED CHICKEN

Easy oven baked chicken with a lovely crispy, flavorful skin.

$^1/_4$ cup Whey Ultimate Bake (50 mL)
  Mix, page 67
2 tsp salt (10 mL)
2 tsp paprika (10 mL)
$^1/_4$ tsp white pepper (1 mL)
3 lbs chicken (back attached) (1.4 kg)
  (about 5 pieces)
$^1/_2$ cup butter, melted (125 mL)

Yield: 5 servings
1 serving
377.5 calories
25.9 g protein
29.0 g fat
1.9 g carbs

In pie dish, combine Whey Ultimate Bake Mix, page 67, salt, paprika and white pepper. Using spoon, coat chicken evenly with mixture. Place skin side down in melted butter in large roasting pan.

Bake in 425°F (220°C) oven 30 minutes. Turn chicken pieces and bake 15 minutes more, or until pieces are fork-tender.

SPICY TOMATO CHICKEN

A very flavorful meal with plenty of vegetables. Add some faux mashed potatoes and you have a super meal.

2 tbsp olive oil (25 mL)
8 chicken breast halves
seasoning salt, to taste
2 tbsp olive oil (25 mL)
1 lb mushrooms, sliced (0.454 kg)
1 small cured Chorizo sausage,
  (about 2 oz (60 g), sliced thinly), OR
  5 slices bacon, cooked and chopped
$^1/_2$ cup chopped onion (125 mL)
2 garlic cloves, minced
7.5 fl. oz tin tomato sauce (213 mL)
$^1/_4$ cup water (50 mL)
1-2 tbsp canned jalapeno pepper,* (15 to 25 mL)
  finely chopped
1 medium tomato, chopped
$^1/_2$ cup chopped fresh parsley (125 mL)
1 avocado, peeled, thinly sliced

Yield: 8 servings
1 serving
273.6 calories
30.2 g protein
13.6 g fat
7.0 g carbs

In large electric frying pan, heat 1 tbsp (15 mL) olive oil at a time. Cut chicken breasts in half. Sauté chicken breasts on both sides until brown. (Sauté half the amount of chicken at a time to prevent stewing the chicken instead; pour off liquid and repeat.) Sprinkle chicken with seasoning salt while cooking. Set chicken aside.

Heat 2 tbsp (25 mL) olive oil. Add mushrooms, Chorizo sausage, onion and garlic. Sauté until mushrooms are tender. Stir in tomato sauce, water and jalapeno pepper. Drain chicken and add in one layer in sauce. Cover and cook on medium heat 20 minutes. Turn chicken over occasionally. Add tomato; cook 5 more minutes. Serve with chopped parsley and sliced avocado.

Helpful Hint: *Mildly spicy with 1 tbsp (15 mL) jalapeno.

BAKED BARBECUE CHICKEN

My dear aunt, Marie Richardson, who is from P.E., South Africa, and now recently lives in Nanaimo, B.C., served us this lovely chicken one evening.

8 chicken breast halves
poultry seasoning, to taste
$^1/_4$ cup olive oil (50 mL)
10 oz can sliced mushrooms, (284 mL)
  OR fresh, sliced mushrooms
chopped parsley for garnish, (optional)
Barbecue Sauce:
1 cup tomato sauce (250 mL)
$^1/_2$ cup water (125 mL)
$^1/_2$ cup chopped onion (125 mL)
$^1/_4$ cup lemon juice (50 mL)
3 tbsp Worcestershire sauce (45 mL)
2 tbsp SPLENDA® Granular (25 mL)
$1^1/_2$ tsp Thickening Agent, page 57, OR (7 mL)
  $^1/_4$ cup soy or spelt flour (50 mL)

Yield: 8 servings
Thickening Agent/soy/spelt
213.1/222.0/225.5 calories
28.5/29.8/29.0 g protein
8.3/8.5/8.4 g fat
4.6/5.6/6.9 g carbs

Season chicken, and if using soy or spelt flour, dredge chicken in flour. In large skillet in half olive oil, brown half the chicken breasts, turning frequently. This takes approximately 15 minutes. Drain skillet and repeat with remaining olive oil and chicken breasts. Place in casserole dish. Pour Barbecue sauce overall. Cover and bake in 350°F (180°C) oven $1^1/_2$ hours. Stir in mushrooms and bake another hour in 300°F (150°C) oven.

Garnish with parsley, if using, and serve over Cauli-Fried Rice, page 53, *More Splendid Low-Carbing* or over spaghetti squash, page 65, *Splendid Low-Carbing,* together with your choice of low-carb vegetables. Serve over brown rice for non low-carbers.

Barbecue Sauce: In medium bowl, combine tomato sauce, water, chopped onion, lemon juice, Worcestershire sauce, SPLENDA® Granular and Thickening Agent, page 57, if using.

Helpful Hints: Marinate chicken overnight in sauce, if desired, to save time the next day. To use the above barbecue sauce for other purposes, simmer 30 minutes in saucepan on stovetop, or microwave 5 minutes in microwave-safe dish. This barbecue sauce will keep in the refrigerator for a while. Heat a portion when needed or add to chicken.

FISH & SHELLFISH

IMPOSSIBLE TUNA PIE

Easy as pie!   Serve with Seasoned Fried Tomatoes, page 86, Splendid Low-Carbing and a leafy salad, if desired. Daniel loves this!

2, 6 oz cans tuna in water, (170 g)
  drained
1 cup old Cheddar cheese, (250 mL)
3 oz cream cheese, diced (90 g)
$^1/_4$ cup chopped green onions (50 mL)
$^3/_4$ cup half-and-half cream (175 mL)
$^3/_4$ cup water (175 mL)
4 eggs
1 cup Whey Ultimate Bake Mix, (250 mL)
  page 67, using whole wheat pastry flour
$^3/_4$ tsp salt (3 mL)
$^1/_2$ tsp baking soda (2 mL)
$^1/_8$ tsp nutmeg (0.5 mL)

Yield: 8 servings
1 serving
270.9 calories
29.3 g protein
14.0 g fat
5.7 g carbs

In medium bowl, combine tuna, Cheddar cheese, cream cheese and green onions. Place in greased 9-inch (23 cm) glass pie dish.

In blender, combine cream, water, eggs, Whey Ultimate Bake Mix, page 67, salt, baking soda and nutmeg. Blend well. Pour over tuna mixture.

Bake in 400°F (200°C) oven 30 minutes; cover with foil and bake another 15 minutes, or until knife inserted in center comes out clean. Allow to cool 5 to 10 minutes before serving.

SPICY SHRIMP

Spicy food speeds up the metabolism. Serve over Cauli-Fried Rice, page 53,
More Splendid Low-Carbing, if desired.

1 cup fresh mushrooms, (250 mL)
   sliced
6 green onions, chopped
2 tbsp butter (25 mL)
1 medium tomato, chopped
1 lb raw medium-size shrimp, (0.454 kg)
   shelled, deveined

Barbecue Sauce:
$^1/_2$ of $5^1/_2$ oz can tomato paste (78 mL)
3 tbsp white vinegar (45 mL)
2 tbsp SPLENDA® Granular (25 mL)
1 tsp Hot Pepper sauce (5 mL)
$^1/_2$ tsp onion salt (2 mL)
$^1/_2$ tsp Worcestershire sauce (2 mL)
$^1/_4$ tsp liquid smoke (1 mL)
$^1/_8$ tsp garlic powder (0.5 mL)
$^1/_8$ tsp black pepper (0.5 mL)

Yield: 4 servings
1 serving
208.2 calories
24.8 g protein
8.1 g fat
7.7 g carbs

In large skillet, sauté mushrooms and green onions in melted butter, until softening. Add tomato and Barbecue Sauce; heat to boiling. Stir in shrimp. Stir frequently and simmer uncovered about 5 minutes, or until shrimp turns pink.

Barbecue Sauce: In small bowl, combine tomato paste, white vinegar, SPLENDA® Granular, Hot Pepper sauce, onion salt, Worcestershire sauce, liquid smoke, garlic powder and black pepper.

Variations: Use a combination of shrimp and scallops. This recipe doubles easily for more servings. Great served in a 2-egg omelet with Cheddar cheese or over Cauli-Fried Rice, page 53, *More Splendid Low-Carbing.*

Helpful Hint: If tomato is very firm, add along with mushrooms and green onions.

SHRIMP STUFFED FILLETS

Covered with lemon sauce and sprinkled with Cheddar cheese.

4 oz canned broken shrimp, (113 g)
  drained
3 tbsp chopped green onion (45 mL)
1 lb Sole or Cod fillets (0.454 kg)
salt and pepper to taste
2 tbsp butter, melted (25 mL)
$^1/_2$ cup grated Cheddar cheese (125 mL)
Lemon Sauce:
$^1/_3$ cup water (75 mL)
$^1/_3$ cup SPLENDA® Granular (75 mL)
2 tbsp lemon juice (25 mL)
$1^1/_2$ tsp instant chicken stock mix (7 mL)
1 tsp grated lemon peel (5 mL)
$^1/_2$ tsp Thickening Agent, page 57 (2 mL)
$^1/_2$ tsp butter (2 mL)

Yield: 4 servings
1 serving
314.4 calories
33.9 g protein
17.7 g fat
3.5 g carbs

In small bowl, mash shrimp lightly and stir in green onion. Divide between fish fillets. Sprinkle with salt and pepper to taste. Roll up.

Place fish seam side down in greased 9 x 13-inch (23 x 33 cm) baking dish. Secure with toothpicks, if necessary. Brush each fillet with butter.

Bake in 425°F (220°C) oven 15 to 20 minutes, or until fish flakes easily. Pour warm lemon Sauce over each fillet and garnish with Cheddar cheese.

Lemon Sauce: In small saucepan, combine water, SPLENDA® Granular, lemon juice, instant chicken stock mix, lemon peel and Thickening Agent, page 57. Whisk and bring to boil. Remove from heat and stir in butter.

BAKED LOBSTER TAILS

Lobster tails, alongside steak, makes for an elegant dinner.

4, 5-oz lobster tails (150 g)
$^1/_2$ cup Healthy Butter, page 96 (125 mL)
 Splendid Low-Carbing, OR butter
 (melted)
2 cloves garlic, crushed

Yield:	4 servings
	1 serving
	333.2 calories
	27.0 g protein
	24.3 g fat
	1.2 g carbs

Use kitchen scissors to split each shell down center only to end of shell. Spread shell apart gently and cut meat down center. Be careful not to cut all the way through. Place finger underneath meat (between meat and cartilage) and bring meat to top of shell. Push shell together so that meat stays on top of shell.

In small bowl, combine melted Healthy Butter, page 96, *Splendid Low-Carbing* and garlic. Brush generously on each lobster. Arrange on cookie sheet. Bake in 550°F (300°C) oven about 7 minutes. Serve with extra melted garlic butter, if desired, for dipping.

DIJON SALMON FILLETS

Salmon is a good source of Omega-3 fatty acid.

4, 6-oz salmon fillets (170 g)
salt and pepper to taste
$^1/_4$ cup unsalted butter, (50 mL)
 softened
2 tbsp lemon juice (25 mL)
2 tbsp chopped green onion (25 mL)
2 tsp Dijon mustard (10 mL)
1 tsp grated lemon peel (5 mL)

Yield:	4 servings
	1 serving
	351.6 calories
	41.3 g protein
	20.6 g fat
	0.9 g carbs

Line cookie sheet with greased foil. Place salmon fillets skin side down. Season fillets with salt and pepper to taste. In small bowl, combine butter, lemon juice, green onion, Dijon mustard and lemon peel. Top each fillet with savory butter. Bake in 400°F (200°C) oven 15 minutes.

PECAN CRUSTED SALMON

This is a fabulous way to serve salmon! Impressive enough for guests.

2 lbs fresh salmon (0.9 kg)
1 tbsp olive oil (15 mL)
1 cup pecans, ground (250 mL)
$1/2$ tsp salt (2 mL)
$1/4$ tsp garlic powder (1 mL)
$1/4$ tsp hot cayenne pepper (1 mL)

Yield: 6 servings
1 serving
385.0 calories
37.9 g protein
25.4 g fat
2.4 g carbs

Brush salmon with oil. In small bowl, combine ground pecans, salt, garlic powder and cayenne pepper. Press pecan mixture over top of salmon. Bake in 375°F (190°C) oven 30 minutes. Broil 12 inches (30 cm) away from heat, about 3 minutes (set timer!). Serve with Horseradish Cream Sauce, page 55, if desired.

TERIYAKI SHRIMP

Tasty and quick!

24 oz frozen salad shrimp (680 g)
2 tbsp olive oil (25 mL)
2 green onions, chopped
Teriyaki Sauce:
3 tbsp SPLENDA® Granular (45 mL)
2 tbsp soy sauce (25 mL)
1 tsp ground ginger (5 mL)
$1/2$ tsp garlic powder (2 mL)
$1/8$ tsp Thickening Agent, page 57 (0.5 mL)

Yield: 4 servings
1 serving
191.3 calories
34.9 g protein
3.0 g fat
3.9 g carbs

Place shrimp in colander and rinse over large bowl under running, cold tap water 1 minute. Allow to soak in water 5 minutes in order to thaw. Drain.

Teriyaki Sauce: In small bowl, combine SPLENDA® Granular, soy sauce, ginger, garlic powder and Thickening Agent, page 57.

In large skillet in olive oil, stir-fry shrimp until liquid accumulates in skillet. Pour off liquid. Add green onions. Stir in Teriyaki Sauce and stir-fry until sauce has thickened. Serve immediately.

TUNA STROGANOFF

Really good flavor – great comfort food! Serve over Cauli-Fried Rice, More Splendid Low-Carbing, page 53, if desired, or over low-carb toast.

1 tbsp butter (15 mL)
$^1/_2$ cup chopped onion (125 mL)
$^1/_2$ cup sour cream (125 mL)
2, 6 oz cans tuna (170 g)
Mushroom Sauce:
$^2/_3$ cup half-and-half cream (150 mL)
$^1/_3$ cup water (75 mL)
2 tbsp butter (25 mL)
$^3/_4$ tsp Thickening Agent, page 57 (3 mL)
  OR 2 tbsp soy or spelt flour (25 mL)
$^1/_2$ tsp salt (2 mL)
$^1/_8$ tsp white pepper (0.5 mL)
$^1/_8$ tsp paprika (0.5 mL)
2 egg yolks, fork beaten
10 oz can sliced mushrooms, (284 mL)
  drained

Yield: 4 servings
1 serving
290.2 calories
22.0 g protein
19.7 g fat
5.5 g carbs

In skillet, melt butter and sauté onion until soft and translucent. Remove from heat.

Mushroom Sauce: In small bowl, combine half-and-half cream and water. Set aside. In double boiler or heavy saucepan, melt butter over low heat. Add soy or spelt flour (if using), salt, pepper and paprika to melted butter. Over low heat, stir together until smooth. Gradually stir in cream and water mixture, using a whisk. Use wooden spoon to incorporate any flour mixture around sides of saucepan. Increase heat to medium. If using Thickening Agent, page 57, instead of soy flour, sprinkle over sauce gradually and whisk in. Stir constantly with whisk, heating to scalding.

In small bowl, stir some of hot liquid into egg yolks. Pour into saucepan and stir over low heat until sauce thickens. Stir in mushrooms. Do not boil. Remove from heat.

Place skillet with cooked onion over medium heat on stove. Stir mushroom sauce and onions together. Stir in sour cream and tuna; heat through.

VEGETABLES

EGGPLANT LASAGNA

This is a fabulous eggplant lasagna. It can also be served as a vegetarian main dish. I love this lasagna – my favorite!

2 large eggplants
2 tbsp olive oil (25 mL)
salt and pepper sprinkle
1.1 lb Ricotta cheese (500 g)
$^3/_4$ cup Mozzarella cheese, cubed (175 mL)
$^1/_3$ cup Parmesan cheese (75 mL)
2 eggs
2 cups tomato sauce (500 mL)
1 tsp dried basil (5 mL)
1 tbsp Parmesan cheese (15 mL)

Yield: 12 servings
1 serving
155.6 calories
10.3 g protein
8.7 g fat
9.5 g carbs

Cut eggplant in $^1/_4$ –inch (0.6 cm) slices. Place slices on greased cookie sheets. Brush lightly with olive oil. Sprinkle with salt and pepper. Cover with foil and bake in 400°F (200°C) oven 20 minutes, or until eggplant slices are soft.

In medium bowl, combine Ricotta cheese, Mozzarella cheese, $^1/_3$ cup (75 mL) Parmesan cheese and eggs. In small bowl combine tomato sauce and basil.

Layer some tomato sauce in bottom of 9 x 13-inch (23 x 33 cm) glass baking dish. Layer eggplant slices and cheese mixture, beginning and ending with tomato sauce. Sprinkle top with 1 tbsp (15 mL) Parmesan cheese.

Bake in 375°F (190°C) oven 40 minutes, or until hot and bubbling.

Helpful Hints: This casserole can be assembled in the morning, refrigerated and cooked many hours later. Peel eggplants, if desired.

SPINACH QUICHE

A delicious recipe given to me by my dear mother-in-law, Kay Eloff, who lives in Cape Town, South Africa. She is one of the most talented people I know. This quiche also makes a great vegetarian entrée, if you leave out the bacon! My husband ordinarily does not like cooked spinach, however, he raved about this.

Crust:
$^1/_2$ cup ground almonds (125 mL)
$^1/_3$ cup grated Parmesan cheese (75 mL)
2 tbsp soy OR spelt flour (25 mL)
3 tbsp unsalted butter, melted (45 mL)
1 egg yolk
Filling:
6 bacon slices
1 whole large leek, cut thin diagonally
1, 10 oz package frozen spinach (300 g)
8 oz light cream cheese, softened (250 g)
1 cup sour cream (250 mL)
5 extra-large eggs, beaten
4 oz feta cheese, crumbled (125 g)
$^1/_2$ cup grated Parmesan cheese (125 mL)

Yield: 10 servings
1 serving
311.1 calories
17.1 g protein
24.3 g fat
5.6 g carbs

Crust: In medium bowl, combine ground almonds, grated Parmesan cheese, soy or spelt flour, melted butter and egg yolk. Press into 9-inch (23 cm) springform pan. Bake in 350°F (180°C) oven 10 minutes.

Filling: In large skillet, cook bacon until just before it gets crisp. Set aside to drain on paper towels. In bacon fat, cook leeks over medium heat until soft. Squeeze liquid out of spinach and add to leeks along with bacon. In food processor or in bowl with electric mixer, process cream cheese. Add sour cream; process. Add eggs one at a time, while processing, until smooth. Stir in feta cheese and half Parmesan cheese. Pour mixture over vegetables and bacon; stir to combine well. Pour over prepared crust.

Bake in 350°F (180°C) oven 50 minutes, or until set. Allow to stand 10 minutes before cutting. Sprinkle remaining Parmesan cheese over top.

Variation: The original recipe had 2, 10-oz packages of frozen spinach in it, as well as the whites only of 2 leeks. (*7.0 g Carbs*)

Helpful Hints: This vegetable quiche makes a nice lunch as well, served with a salad and fresh low-carb bread.

EGGPLANT ALMONDINE

This is my top favorite way to eat this vegetable. It tastes like the eggplant has been breaded with real fine breadcrumbs.

$1^1/_4$ lbs eggplant* (0.567 kg)
1 extra-large egg, fork beaten
1 tbsp water (15 mL)
$1^1/_8$ cups ground almonds (275 mL)
$^1/_4$ cup olive oil (50 mL)
seasoning salt, to taste**

Yield: 8 servings
1 serving
182.1 calories
4.8 g protein
16.0 g fat
5.6 g carbs

Wash eggplant surface well and cut into thin slices. In small bowl, combine egg and water. Place ground almonds on a dinner plate. Dip eggplant slices in egg wash and cover in ground almonds on both sides. In large skillet, fry in olive oil until golden brown underneath. Sprinkle surface with seasoning salt, flip and cook other side as well, seasoning also to taste. Be careful not to burn them. They cook fairly quickly, especially, when a lid is placed over the skillet.

Helpful Hint: *I removed the inedible parts of the eggplant, before I weighed it. **Hys® seasoning salt is the one I used.

BACON FRIED MUSHROOMS

My son, Daniel, loves these mushrooms.

6 slices bacon
1 cup chopped onion (250 mL)
$1^1/_2$ lbs fresh mushrooms (0.680 kg)
$^1/_2$ tsp salt (2 mL)
$^1/_4$ tsp white pepper (1 mL)

Yield: 6 servings
1 serving
75.1 calories
7.4 g protein
2.2 g fat
6.1 g carbs

In large electric frying pan, fry bacon until crisp. Add onion to bacon drippings. Fry until soft. Wash and slice mushrooms; add to pan. Stir-fry mushrooms until tender. Sprinkle with salt and pepper.

Helpful Hint: Using only $^1/_2$ cup (125 mL) chopped onion, brings the carb count down one gram.

GREEN BEANS WITH PIZZAZ

Special green beans that will liven up any meal.

$1^1/_4$ lbs cut green beans, (0.567 kg)
  (frozen)
2 slices bacon, chopped
$^1/_4$ cup chopped onion (50 mL)
3 tbsp red wine vinegar (45 mL)
2 tbsp SPLENDA® Granular (25 mL)

Yield: 6 servings
1 serving
48.7 calories
3.7 g protein
0.8 g fat
6.4 g carbs

In large nonstick saucepan, in 1-inch (2.5 cm) boiling water, add green beans and bring quickly to second boil. Reduce heat and simmer 4 to 6 minutes, until tender. Drain beans in colander.

Return saucepan to stove top and cook bacon until fat begins to render. Add chopped onion and cook until tender. Add drained green beans to saucepan and cook until hot, stirring occasionally. Add red wine vinegar and SPLENDA® Granular. Allow vinegar to evaporate, 1 to 2 minutes; serve.

PEPPERY BROCCOLI

Spicy, colorful side dish.

1 tbsp olive oil (15 mL)
$^1/_2$ tsp crushed garlic (2 mL)
$^1/_8$ tsp crushed red pepper (0.5 mL)
3 cups chopped broccoli (750 mL)
1 cup red pepper strips (250 mL)
$^1/_4$ tsp black pepper (1 mL)
$^1/_8$ tsp salt (0.5 mL)

Yield: 6 servings
1 serving
40.6 calories
1.6 g protein
2.5 g fat
2.8 g carbs

In large skillet or electric frying pan, in olive oil, cook garlic and crushed red pepper very briefly. Add broccoli and red pepper strips. Stir-fry about 5 minutes, or until vegetables are tender crisp. Sprinkle with black pepper and salt.

Helpful Hints: Don't throw away broccoli stalks, except for the very tough ends. Peel outside of stalks and chop coarsely

IMPOSSIBLE VEGETABLE PIE

This delicious idea came from my dear friend, Jeanne Lobsinger, from Vernon, British Columbia, who is a fabulous cook.

2 cups each broccoli and (500 mL)
 cauliflower, OR use broccoflower
$^1/_2$ cup onion, chopped (125 mL)
1 small red pepper, chopped
1 cup grated Cheddar cheese (250 mL)
$^3/_4$ cup Ultimate Bake (175 mL)
 Mix, page 67, (Whey, OR Soy UBM)
$^3/_4$ cup whipping cream (175 mL)
$^1/_2$ cup water (125 mL)
3 eggs, fork beaten
$^3/_4$ tsp salt (3 mL)

Yield: 8 servings
1 serving
213.2 calories
11.5 g protein
14.9 g fat
7.3 g carbs

Grease 2-quart (2 L) casserole dish. Add broccoli, cauliflower, onion and red pepper. Cover with cheese. In medium bowl, combine Ultimate Bake Mix, page 67, whipping cream, water, eggs and salt. Pour over vegetables and bake in 400°F (200°C) oven 40 minutes.

YELLOW SQUASH CASSEROLE

A lovely way to dress up plain squash.

2 cups cooked yellow squash (500 mL)
1 cup grated Cheddar cheese, (250 mL)
 divided
2 eggs, fork beaten
$^1/_2$ cup water (125 mL)
$^1/_4$ cup Ultimate Bake Mix, (50 mL)
 page 67, (Whey, OR Soy UBM)
$^1/_4$ cup whipping cream (50 mL)
3 tbsp butter, melted (45 mL)
1 tbsp minced, dehydrated onion (15 mL)
1 tbsp SPLENDA® Granular (15 mL)
$^1/_2$ tsp salt (2 mL)
$^1/_8$ tsp white pepper (0.5 mL)

Yield: 10 servings
1 serving
142.2 calories
5.8 g protein
10.9 g fat
5.3 g carbs

In large bowl, combine squash, half Cheddar cheese, eggs, water, Ultimate Bake Mix, page 67, whipping cream, butter, onion, SPLENDA® Granular, salt and pepper. Stir well. Pour into greased, deep 9-inch (23 cm) glass pie dish. Sprinkle with remaining Cheddar cheese. Bake in 350°F (180°C) oven 40 minutes.

MISCELLANEOUS

ANY-FLAVOR SYRUP

This is a useful recipe to produce slightly thicker syrups. It's lovely poured over fruit salad too.

1 cup Da Vinci® Sugar Free (250 mL)
  Any Fruity Flavor Syrup
$^1/_2$ cup water (125 mL)
1 tsp lemon juice (5 mL)
2 SPLENDA® packets
1 tsp Thickening Agent, (5 mL)
  page 57
2 tsp butter (10 mL)
*1 cup fruit, such as berries, OR (250 mL)
  peaches, etc., (optional)

> *Yield:* $1^1/_2$ cups (375 mL)
> $^1/_4$ cup (50 mL) per serving
> 13.0 calories
> 0.0 g protein
> 1.3 g fat
> *0.5 g carbs*

Into medium saucepan, pour Da Vinci® Sugar Free Syrup, water, lemon juice and SPLENDA®. Sprinkle Thickening Agent, page 57, over and whisk, bringing syrup to boiling point.

Remove from heat. Stir in butter. Sieve, if necessary. Stir in fresh fruit, if using.

Variation: **Da Vinci® Alternative:** Use water and sugar free Kool-Aid® to taste.

Helpful Hints: *If using frozen fruit, add at the beginning of cooking the syrup. Heat to boiling.

This Syrup makes a pretty fruit glaze.

CONFECTIONER'S SUGAR SUBSTITUTE

This is an easier recipe than the one in my previous books.

2$^1/_4$ cups SPLENDA® Granular (550 mL)
1$^1/_3$ cups whole milk powder* (325 mL)
$^2/_3$ cup vanilla whey protein (150 mL)

Yield: 4 cups (1 L)
1 tbsp (15 mL) per serving
19.7 calories
1.4 g protein
0.7 g fat
1.9 g carbs

In large bowl, combine SPLENDA® Granular, whole milk powder and vanilla whey protein.

Helpful Hint: *Skim milk powder may be used instead, however, blend finely in blender first, before combining with remaining ingredients.

HEALTHY BUTTER

This is a clever way to make butter healthier and higher in monounsaturated fats.
The taste is just like butter, plus it spreads easily straight from the refrigerator.
My dear friend, Mary Converse from Great Falls, Montana gave me this idea.

1 lb butter, softened (0.454 kg)
1$^1/_2$ cups light-tasting olive oil (375 mL)

Yield: 3 cups (750 mL)
1 tsp (5 mL) per serving
42.5 calories
0.0 g protein
4.8 g fat
0.0 g carbs

In blender, process butter and olive oil until soft, creamy and smooth. Turn out into plastic bowl with lid and refrigerate until firm.

Helpful Hints: I usually double this recipe as it lasts long in the refrigerator. Choose an olive oil that has no perceptible taste, so that it doesn't overpower the taste of the butter. If per chance the olive oil overpowers the butter taste, then use that Healthy Butter for frying and cooking.

CRÈME FRAICHE

Lovely sweetened whipped topping for serving with desserts or for garnishing desserts. It holds up better than plain whipped cream and tastes better. Double Thickening agent, page 57, for thicker Crème Fraiche.

1 cup whipping cream (250 mL)
$^1/_2$ cup SPLENDA® Granular (125 mL)
$^1/_4$ tsp Thickening Agent, page 57 (1 mL)
  (optional)
$^2/_3$ cup regular sour cream, OR (150 mL)
  nonfat sour cream
$^1/_2$ tsp vanilla extract (2 mL)

> **Yield:** $2^1/_8$ cups (525 mL)
> 2 tbsp (25 mL) per serving
> 56.2 calories
> 0.5 g protein
> 5.4 g fat
> **1.5 g carbs**

In food processor, on low speed, process whipping cream with SPLENDA® Granular. While processing, sprinkle in Thickening Agent, page 57, if using, through feed tube. Process until thick. Add sour cream and vanilla extract; process on medium high speed just until combined. It will keep at least one week or longer in the refrigerator.

Variation: **Lower Carb Alternative:** Omit SPLENDA® Granular. Use $^1/_2$ tsp (2 mL) to $^3/_4$ tsp (3 mL) Thickening Agent, page 57. Use $^1/_4$ cup (50 mL) Da Vinci® Sugar Free Syrup such as Vanilla or French Vanilla instead of SPLENDA® Granular. Process whipping cream and Thickening Agent, page 57, until thick. Add syrup along with sour cream; process.
2 tbsp (25 mL) per serving: (53.6 calories, 0.5 g protein, 5.4 g fat, **0.8 g carbs**)

Helpful Hints: Thickening Agent, page 57, makes Crème Fraiche firmer and easier to garnish desserts using a pastry bag.

This topping is wonderful on fresh fruit salad or fresh strawberries. In my opinion, it tastes better than sweetened whipped cream. Recipe may easily be doubled or halved.

Half this recipe will suffice as a topping for a cheesecake.
Yield: 12 servings. 1 serving: (42.0 calories, 0.4 g protein, 4.1 g fat, **1.1 g carbs**)

BREAD-SAUSAGE STUFFING

A more traditional stuffing.

1 lb seasoned sausage meat (0.454 kg)
1 cup finely chopped onion (250 mL)
5 slices low-carb bread torn, each about
  5 grams carbohydrate
2 eggs, fork beaten
$^1/_4$ cup water (50 mL)
2 tsp dried parsley (10 mL)
$^1/_4$ tsp instant chicken stock mix (1 mL)
$^1/_4$ tsp salt (1 mL)
$^1/_4$ tsp black pepper (1 mL)

Yield: 10 servings
1 serving
209.6 calories
10.0 g protein
16.1 g fat
5.0 g carbs

In large skillet, cook sausage meat. Pour off excess fat. Add onion; cook until soft.

In large bowl, combine cooked sausage and onion, bread, eggs, water, parsley, instant chicken stock mix, salt and pepper. Use to stuff poultry.

HORSERADISH CREAM SAUCE

This sauce is fabulous with fish or roast beef.

$^1/_3$ cup whipping cream (75 mL)
$^1/_4$ cup mayonnaise (50 mL)
2 tbsp horseradish (25 mL)
1 tbsp mustard (15 mL)
1 tsp SPLENDA® Granular (5 mL)
$^1/_8$ tsp salt (0.5 mL)
$^1/_8$ tsp white pepper (0.5 mL)
$^1/_8$ tsp hot cayenne pepper (0.5 mL)

Yield: $^3/_4$ cup (175 mL)
1 tbsp (15 mL) per serving
30.5 calories
0.2 g protein
3.1 g fat
0.5 g carbs

In medium bowl, combine whipping cream, mayonnaise, horseradish, mustard, SPLENDA® Granular, salt, pepper and cayenne pepper. Refrigerate.

CONDENSED MILK

Be prepared for a delicious surprise – very similar in consistency and taste to the real thing! This recipe will be useful in some of your old favorite desserts.

$^1/_3$ cup whipping cream (75 mL)
$^1/_3$ cup butter, softened (75 mL)
3 tbsp water (45 mL)
$^1/_2$ tsp vanilla extract (2 mL)
$^2/_3$ cup SPLENDA® Granular (150 mL)
$^1/_3$ cup vanilla whey protein (75 mL)
$^1/_3$ cup whole milk powder (75 mL)
$^1/_8$ tsp Thickening Agent, (0.5 mL)
  page 57

> **Yield:** $1^1/_8$ cups (275 mL)
> 1 tbsp (15 mL) per serving
> 65.8 calories˙
> 2.0 g protein
> 5.6 g fat
> **2.0 g carbs**

In blender, place whipping cream, butter, water, vanilla extract, SPLENDA® Granular, vanilla whey protein, whole milk powder and Thickening Agent, page 57. Blend until smooth.

Lower Carb Alternative: Use 2 tbsp (25 mL) whipping cream, 1 tbsp (15 mL) water and use $^1/_3$ cup (75 mL) Caramel, French Vanilla or Dulce De Leche Da Vinci® Sugar Free Syrup. Omit SPLENDA® Granular, however, add 1 SPLENDA® packet, if desired. Increase Thickening Agent to $^1/_4$ tsp (1 mL). 1 tbsp (15mL): (53.4 calories, 2.0 g protein, 4.79 g fat (77.8%), **1.0 g carbs**)

Helpful Hints: Skim milk powder may be used instead. Blend in blender until fine in texture, then measure.

Some health food stores actually sell a finely ground skim milk powder, similar to the whole milk powder.

THICKENING AGENT

This is useful to use instead of pure cornstarch or flour in thickening sauces.

$8^1/_2$ tsp xanthan gum (42 mL)
$4^1/_2$ tsp guar gum (22 mL)
$2^1/_4$ tsp corn starch (11 mL)

> **Yield:** $^1/_3$ cup (75 mL)
> 1 tsp (5 mL) per serving
> 1.5 calories
> 0.0 g protein
> 0.0 g fat
> **0.4 g carbs**

In small plastic container with lid, combine xanthan gum, guar gum and cornstarch; seal. Store at room temperature.

Helpful Hints: Substitute Thickening Agent for cornstarch, using $^1/_4$ as much and substitute Thickening Agent for flour, using $^1/_8$ as much to achieve approximately the same results.

This Thickening Agent must be used in small quantities to avoid a "gummy" texture. For instance, do not use in quantities greater than $^1/_2$ tsp (2 mL) for thickening sauces for stir-fried vegetables.

You may use only guar gum or only xanthan gum, if one or the other is not available.

Thickening Agent is utilized frequently throughout this cookbook; however, if you would like the convenience of a commercial product, then use "ThickenThin not/Starch" by Expert Foods (http://expertfoods.com). Things come out more or less the same.

EASY BERRY JAMS

Use blueberries, blackberries or raspberries and a suitable sugar free syrup to further enhance the fruit flavor.

Strawberry Jam:
4 envelopes unflavored gelatin
$1^1/_2$ cups Da Vinci® Sugar Free (375 mL)
  Strawberry Syrup
2 lbs frozen strawberries, (0.9 kg)
  unsweetened
1 tbsp lemon juice (15 mL)
1 cup SPLENDA® Granular (250 mL)
$^1/_4$ tsp butter (1 mL)

Yield: 5 cups (1.25 L) 1 tsp (5 mL) per serving 2.2 calories 0.1 g protein 0.0 g fat **0.4 g carbs**

In small bowl, combine gelatin and 1 cup (250 mL) Da Vinci® Sugar Free Strawberry Syrup.

In large saucepan, combine strawberries, lemon juice and $^1/_2$ cup (125 mL) Da Vinci® Sugar Free Strawberry Syrup. Over medium heat, cook strawberries until softening. Crush fruit with potato masher. Stir in SPLENDA® Granular. Stir in gelatin mixture. Bring to full rolling boil, while stirring. Add butter. Boil hard 1 minute. Remove from heat and skim foam off with long-handled spoon. Fill sterilized jam jars and seal. Allow to cool. Refrigerate sealed up to 6 months or freeze for longer storage.

Variations: **Bumbleberry Jam:** Substitute a 2 lb (0.9 kg) combination of blackberries, blueberries and raspberries – sometimes one can buy this combination in the frozen section of the supermarket. Omit lemon juice. (**0.5 g Carbs**)

Raspberry Jam: Use 2 lbs (0.9 kg) raspberries. (**0.3 g Carbs**)

Blueberry Jam: Use 2 lbs (0.9 kg) blueberries. Omit lemon juice. (**0.5 g Carbs**)

Huckleberry Jam: Use 2 lbs (0.9 kg) huckleberries. Omit lemon juice. (**0.5 g Carbs**)

Da Vinci® Alternative: Use 1 package sugar free Kool-Aid® (or more, to taste) of a matching flavor to the fruit, water instead of Da Vinci® Sugar Free Syrup and an extra cup (250 mL) SPLENDA® Granular, or to taste. (**0.6 g Carbs**)

FLAVORED SWEET BUTTERS

Many uses for these wonderful butters: think of spreading muffins, pancakes, low-carb toast, crackers, etc. with this sweet butter, instead of fruit spread.

Cinnamon Butter:
$^1/_2$ cup Healthy Butter,* page 53 (125 mL)
8 SPLENDA® packets
2 tbsp whipping cream (25 mL)
1 tbsp cinnamon (15 mL)

Yield: $^1/_2$ cup (125 mL)
1 tsp (5 mL) per serving
39.2 calories
0.1 g protein
4.2 g fat
0.4 g carbs

In food processor with sharp blade, process Healthy Butter, page 53, SPLENDA®, whipping cream and cinnamon until smooth. Keep refrigerated.

Variations: **Apple Cinnamon Butter:** Use Da Vinci® Sugar Free Green Apple Syrup instead of whipping cream. (*0.4 g Carbs*)

Apple Butter: Substitute $1^1/_2$ tbsp (22 mL) Da Vinci® Sugar Free Green Apple Syrup for whipping cream and omit cinnamon. (*0.3 g Carbs*)

Create-a-Flavor Sweet Butter: Use $1^1/_2$ tbsp (22 mL) any flavor Da Vinci® Sugar Free Syrup. (*0.3 g Carbs*)

Helpful Hint: *One may use regular butter (heated in microwave oven 25 seconds), however, it will be harder to spread the flavored sweet butter once chilled. Remove from refrigerator 15 minutes, before using.

LEMON CURD

Use instead of jam on low-carb toast or atop fresh, summer berries. This recipe can easily be doubled.

3 large egg yolks
$^1/_4$ cup lemon juice, (50 mL)
  freshly squeezed (1-2 lemons)
6 tbsp SPLENDA® Granular (90 mL)
1 tbsp grated lemon peel (15 mL)
4 tbsp unsalted butter (50 mL)

> **Yield:** $^2/_3$ cup (150 mL)
> 1 tbsp (15 mL) per serving
> 64.1 calories
> 0.9 g protein
> 6.1 g fat
> **1.5 g carbs**

In double boiler, combine egg yolks, lemon juice SPLENDA® Granular and lemon peel. Cook until mixture is fairly thick. Remove from heat and stir in butter, one tablespoon (15 mL) at a time, until smooth.

Pour into small container. Cover surface with plastic wrap (to prevent a skin from forming) and refrigerate.

SPREADABLE CREAM CHEESE

Use any flavor Da Vinci® Sugar Free Syrup.

6 oz regular cream cheese, (180 g)
2 tbsp Da Vinci® Sugar Free (25 mL)
  Syrup (any flavor)

> **Yield:** 6 oz (180 g)
> 1 oz (30 g) per serving
> 94.5 calories
> 2.8 g protein
> 8.9 g fat
> **0.9 g carbs**

In food processor or blender, process cream cheese and Da Vinci® Sugar Free Syrup, until smooth. Keep refrigerated.

Variation: **Da Vinci® Alternative:** Use water, vanilla or other flavored extract and SPLENDA® Granular to taste.

BREADS, BAKE MIXES & BAKING

RASPBERRY MUFFINS

A pretty muffin that tastes high carb, and is so good warm out of the oven!

$2^1/_4$ cups Vital Ultimate Bake (550 mL)
  Mix,* page 67
$^1/_2$ cup SPLENDA® Granular (125 mL)
1 tbsp baking powder (15 mL)
$^1/_8$ tsp salt (0.5 mL)
2 tbsp butter (25 mL)
1 cup fresh or frozen raspberries (250 mL)
2 eggs
$^1/_2$ cup Da Vinci® Sugar Free (125 mL)
  Vanilla Syrup
$^1/_3$ cup olive oil (75 mL)
2 tbsp whipping cream (25 mL)

> **Yield:** 12 muffins
> 1 muffin
> 204.0 calories
> 7.4 g protein
> 15.5 g fat
> **8.4 g carbs**

In large bowl, combine Vital Ultimate Bake Mix, page 67, SPLENDA® Granular, baking powder and salt. Rub in butter. Fold in raspberries. In medium bowl, beat eggs with fork and stir in Da Vinci® Sugar Free Vanilla Syrup, olive oil and whipping cream. Stir into dry ingredients, just until moistened. Fill 12 greased muffin cups. Bake in 400°F (200°C) oven 15 minutes, or until tops are golden brown.

Variation: **Da Vinci® Alternative:** Use water and 2 tsp (10 mL) vanilla extract instead of Da Vinci® Sugar Free Vanilla Syrup. Increase sweetness by an extra $^1/_4$ cup (50 mL) SPLENDA® Granular. (*8.9 g Carbs*) To reduce carbs slightly, use 8 SPLENDA® packets instead of the granular option. (*8.0 g Carbs*)

Pineapple Raspberry Muffins: Use Da Vinci® Sugar Free Pineapple Syrup.

Helpful Hints: *Vital Ultimate Bake Mix with oat flour instead of spelt flour reduces the carb count by almost 2 grams (*6.7 g carbs*). In main recipe, I used ground almonds and all-purpose flour in the Vital Ultimate Bake Mix, page 67, producing moist, dense, soft cake-like muffins. Spelt flour would work well too.

BANANALESS BANANA MUFFINS

The recipe for these delicious, flourless muffins was given to me by a man who enjoys my cookbooks: Kevin A. Sapp of Cary, NC. His sons love the muffins, as do my much older sons – actually, we all like them!

8 oz light, OR regular cream (250 g)
  cheese, softened
2 eggs
1$^1/_3$ cups ground almonds (325 mL)
$^1/_2$ cup SPLENDA® Granular (125 mL)
$^1/_3$ cup vanilla whey protein (75 mL)
$^1/_4$ cup Da Vinci® Sugar Free (50 mL)
  Banana Syrup
$^1/_4$ cup olive oil (50 mL)
1 tbsp whipping cream (15 mL)
2 tsp baking powder (10 mL)
$^1/_2$ tsp baking soda (2 mL)
1 tsp vanilla extract (5 mL)
1 tsp cinnamon (5 mL)

Yield: 12 muffins
1 muffin
188.0 calories
6.9 g protein
16.4 g fat
3.0 g carbs

In food processor or in bowl with electric mixer, process cream cheese until smooth. Add eggs, ground almonds, SPLENDA® Granular, vanilla whey protein, Da Vinci® Sugar Free Banana Syrup, olive oil, whipping cream, baking powder, baking soda, vanilla extract and cinnamon; process.

Fill 12 greased muffin cups. Bake in 350°F (180°C) oven 18 to 20 minutes, or until golden brown and cake tester comes out clean.

Variations: **Create-a-Flavor Muffin:** Use any appropriate flavor Da Vinci® Sugar Free Syrup. Omit cinnamon, where it makes sense to leave it out. This muffin, using regular cream cheese, can actually be used on a "fat fast."

Fruity Muffins: Use Da Vinci® Sugar Free Vanilla or French Vanilla Syrup and add 1 cup (250 mL) fruit such as blueberries (***4.5 g Carbs***), peaches (***4.4 g Carbs***) or raspberries (***3.7 g Carbs***). You can try fruity flavors of Da Vinci® Sugar Free Syrups to match the fruit, however, you could wind up with a very colorful muffin with some of them. Children might actually enjoy that!

Banana Nut Muffins: Add $^3/_4$ cup (175 mL) chopped, fresh walnuts or pecans. (***3.6 g Carbs***)

Da Vinci® Alternative: Use water, $^2/_3$ cup (150 mL) SPLENDA® Granular and 1 tsp (5 mL) banana extract instead of vanilla extract. (***3.4 g Carbs***)

AUNTY MARIE'S BLUEBERRY MUFFINS

My aunt, Marie Richardson, often makes these muffins to everyone's delight!
The high-carb version of this recipe is out of this world, however, these are a
good low-carb version of her muffins. Ever since I was a young child, I
remember my aunt's fabulous baking.

$^1/_4$ cup butter, softened (50 mL)
2 eggs
1 cup sour cream (250 mL)
$^2/_3$ cup SPLENDA® Granular (150 mL)
2 tbsp Da Vinci® Sugar Free (25 mL)
  Orange Syrup
2 tsp grated lemon peel (10 mL)
$1^3/_4$ cups Whey, OR Vital (425 mL)
  Ultimate Bake Mix,* page 67
1 tsp baking soda (5 mL)
1 cup frozen blueberries (250 mL)
1 tbsp SPLENDA® Granular, (15 mL)
$^1/_2$ tsp lemon peel (2 mL)

> **Yield:** 12 muffins
> 1 muffin/ Whey/Vital UBM
> 160.8/169.6 calories
> 7.6/6.5 g protein
> 10.7/12.1 g fat
> ***8.2/8.4 g carbs***

In food processor with sharp blade or in bowl with electric mixer, process butter and eggs. Add sour cream, $^2/_3$ cup (150 mL) SPLENDA® Granular, Da Vinci® Sugar Free Orange Syrup and 2 tsp (10 mL) lemon peel; process.

In medium bowl, combine Whey Ultimate Bake Mix, page 67 and baking soda. Stir in sour cream mixture. Fold in blueberries. Fill 12 greased muffin cups $^2/_3$ full.

In small bowl, stir together SPLENDA® Granular and $^1/_2$ tsp (2 mL) lemon peel. Sprinkle tops of muffins with this mixture. Bake in 375°F (190°C) oven 20 to 25 minutes, or until cake tester comes out clean. Cool 5 minutes in pan.

Variation:* Cranberry-Pecan Muffins:** Use $^1/_2$ cup (125 mL) frozen cranberries (chopped finely in food processor) and $^1/_2$ cup (125 mL) chopped pecans. Increase SPLENDA® Granular to $^3/_4$ cup (175 mL). (8.1/8.3 g Carbs***)

Helpful Hints: *Muffins are moister with Vital Ultimate Bake Mix, page 67. Carbs will be reduced by 1.2 grams, if using Vital Oat Ultimate Bake Mix (***7.2 g Carbs***). My aunt's original recipe called for 2 tbsp (25 mL) orange juice from concentrate, instead of the sugar free syrup. Refrigerate or freeze muffins after a day. Recipe was successful using Nut-Free Oat Ultimate Bake Mix, page 68. (***7.2 g Carbs***) I used Da Vinci® Sugar Free Banana Syrup, however, 1 tsp (5 mL) banana extract and water to equal 2 tbsp (25 mL) would work nicely as well.

BROWNIE LOAF

No flour in this lovely, moist, very chocolate-y loaf, however, one would never guess. The zucchini is not detectable!

1$^1/_2$ cups ground hazelnuts (375 mL)
1$^1/_2$ cups SPLENDA® Granular (375 mL)
$^3/_4$ cup chocolate whey protein (175 mL)
6 tbsp cocoa (90 mL)
1$^1/_2$ tsp baking powder (7 mL)
$^3/_4$ tsp baking soda (3 mL)
$^3/_4$ tsp cinnamon (3 mL)
2 extra-large eggs, fork beaten
1$^1/_8$ cups grated zucchini (275 mL)
1$^1/_8$ cups sour cream (275 mL)
6 tbsp olive oil (90 mL)
1$^1/_2$ tsp vanilla extract (7 mL)
Chocolate Fudge Frosting, page 95

Yield: 18 slices
1 slice
192.3 calories
5.8 g protein
16.7 g fat
5.6 g carbs

In large bowl, combine ground hazelnuts, SPLENDA® Granular, chocolate whey protein, cocoa, baking powder, baking soda and cinnamon. In medium bowl, combine eggs, zucchini, sour cream, olive oil and vanilla extract. Stir into dry ingredients, just until combined. Pour into 9 x 5 x 3-inch (2 L) loaf pan lined with wax paper and sprayed with nonstick cooking spray.

Bake in 350°F (180°C) oven 55 minutes to an hour, or until cake tester comes out clean. Remove loaf and carefully remove wax paper. Spread Chocolate Fudge Frosting, page 95, over top of loaf.

Chocolate Fudge Frosting: Prepare frosting as directed on page 95.

Helpful Hints: Another frosting idea is to melt a sugar free chocolate bar with 2 tbsp (25 mL) Healthy Butter, page 53, and spread over loaf. Carbs will be reduced slightly. (**4.6 g Carbs**)

This Brownie Loaf is lovely chilled as well. It is a cross between a brownie and a rich, chocolate muffin. For those, who are not aware: $^1/_8$ cup = 2 tbsp (25 mL).

PUMPKIN SPICE LOAF

You can feel proud to serve this delicious, moist loaf anytime. My youngest son, Jonathan, almost single-handedly polished off the Apple Spice Loaf, however, the Pumpkin Spice Loaf is definitely my favorite of the two.

$1^1/_2$ cups ground almonds (375 mL)
$1^1/_2$ cups SPLENDA® Granular (375 mL)
$3/_4$ cup vanilla whey protein (175 mL)
6 tbsp vital wheat gluten (90 mL)
$1^1/_2$ tsp pumpkin pie spice (7 mL)
$1^1/_2$ tsp baking powder (7 mL)
$3/_4$ tsp baking soda (3 mL)
2 extra-large eggs, fork beaten
1 cup canned pumpkin, (250 mL)
 (unsweetened)
$1/_2$ cup sour cream (125 mL)
6 tbsp olive oil (90 mL)
$1^1/_2$ tsp vanilla extract (7 mL)
Cream Cheese Frosting:
4 oz light cream cheese, softened (125 g)
$1/_3$ cup SPLENDA® Granular (75 mL)
2 tbsp butter, softened (25 mL)
1 tbsp whipping cream (15 mL)
1 tsp vanilla extract (5 mL)

Yield: 18 slices
1 slice
182.8 calories
8.2 g protein
14.3 g fat
5.1 g carbs

In large bowl, combine ground almonds, SPLENDA® Granular, vanilla whey protein, vital wheat gluten, pumpkin pie spice, baking powder and baking soda. In medium bowl, combine eggs pumpkin, sour cream, olive oil and vanilla extract. Stir into dry ingredients, just until combined.

Pour into a 9 x 5 x 3-inch (2 L) loaf pan lined with wax paper and sprayed with nonstick cooking spray. Bake in 350°F (180°C) oven 55 minutes, or until cake tester comes out clean. Remove loaf and carefully remove wax paper. Frost cooled loaf. (The wax paper trick is useful to prevent loaf from sticking to old and worn loaf pans. If yours is brand new and nonstick, then skip the wax paper.)

Cream Cheese Frosting: In food processor with sharp blade or in blender, process cream cheese, SPLENDA® Granular, butter, whipping cream and vanilla extract until smooth.

Variation: Apple Spice Loaf with Frosting: Omit pumpkin. Substitute $1/_2$ cup (125 mL) unsweetened applesauce and use $1/_4$ cup (50 mL) sour cream. (**5.2 g Carbs**) This loaf goes well with Cinnamon Butter, page 59.

CRANBERRY ORANGE LOAF

You can proudly serve this beautiful, flavorful and moist loaf to your guests. They will never guess it is a low-carb loaf. The fresh loaf has a light, crispy crust, which is rather nice.

$2^1/_4$ cups Whey Ultimate Bake (550 mL)
  Mix, page 67
2 tsp baking powder (10 mL)
$^1/_2$ tsp baking soda (2 mL)
$^1/_4$ tsp salt (1 mL)
3 tbsp grated orange peel (45 mL)
$1^1/_4$ cups frozen cranberries, (300 mL)
  (unsweetened)
$^1/_4$ cup olive oil (50 mL)
2 tbsp butter, melted (25 mL)
1 egg
1 cup SPLENDA® Granular (250 mL)
$^2/_3$ cup Da Vinci® Sugar Free Orange Syrup (150 mL)

Yield: 18 slices
1 slice
114.7 calories
5.5 g protein
7.4 g fat
6.1 g carbs

In large bowl, combine Whey Ultimate Bake Mix, page 67, baking powder, baking soda and salt. Stir in grated orange peel. Fold in frozen cranberries.

In food processor or in bowl with electric mixer, process olive oil, butter and egg. Add SPLENDA® Granular; process. Add to cranberry mixture, along with Da Vinci® Sugar Free Orange Syrup. Stir with wooden spoon, just until all dry ingredients are incorporated. Pour into 9 x 5 x 3-inch (2 L) loaf pan lined with wax paper and sprayed with nonstick cooking spray. Bake in 350°F (180°C) oven 40 minutes, or until cake tester comes out clean. Remove loaf and carefully remove wax paper.

Variation: **Da Vinci® Alternative:** Use 2 tbsp (25 mL) orange juice concentrate, $^1/_2$ cup (125 mL) extra SPLENDA® Granular, $^1/_2$ cup (125 mL) water and $^1/_2$ tsp (2 mL) orange extract. (***7.6 g Carbs***) Alternatively, use 8 SPLENDA® packets (instead of 1 cup (250 mL) SPLENDA® Granular) and $^1/_2$ cup (125 mL) extra SPLENDA® Granular for the sweetener in this Da Vinci® Alternative recipe: (***6.5 g Carbs***)

Helpful Hint: When formulating the Whey Ultimate Bake Mix, page 67, I used all purpose flour, however, spelt flour would work as well. Typically, bake mixes formulated with spelt flour as opposed to all-purpose flour, produce a slightly denser baked product, similar to baking with whole wheat flour.

ULTIMATE BAKE MIX

Substitute cup-for-cup for all-purpose flour. Regular sugar and white flour recipes will have carbs reduced by at least 60 %, if SPLENDA® is used as well.

Vital Ultimate Bake Mix:

$1^1/_2$ cups ground almonds, OR (375 mL)
  ground hazelnuts, pecans or walnuts
1 cup spelt, OR all-purpose, (250 mL)
  whole wheat, whole wheat pastry flour,
  or oat flour* (last two have fewer carbs)
$^1/_2$ cup vital wheat gluten (125 mL)

> **Yield:** $2^3/_4$ cups (675 mL)
> $^1/_4$ cup (50 mL) per serving
> 139.5 calories
> 8.2 g protein
> 8.0 g fat
> **8.4 g carbs**

In medium bowl, combine ground almonds (hazelnuts, pecans or walnuts), spelt flour (all-purpose, whole wheat flour, whole wheat pastry or oat flour) and vital wheat gluten; stir well. With all bake mixes, add liquid in your own recipes very cautiously, withholding at least $^1/_2$ cup (125 mL) and adding it as necessary.

Variations: **Whey Ultimate Bake Mix (soy-free):** Combine 1 cup (250 mL) ground almonds or hazelnuts, etc., 1 cup (250 mL) spelt, all-purpose flour, whole wheat flour, or whole wheat pastry flour, etc., $^2/_3$ cup (150 mL) natural whey protein powder and 6 tbsp (90 mL) vital wheat gluten. *Yield:* 3 cups (750 mL), $^1/_4$ cup (50 mL)/serv. **With spelt:** 124.4 cal., 10.1 g protein, 5.6 g fat, *7.9 g carbs*. **With whole wheat pastry flour:** 116.3 cal., 9.8 g protein, 5.6 g fat, *6.4 g carbs*.

Oat Ultimate Bake Mix: Mix 1 cup (250 mL) ground hazelnuts or ground almonds, 1 cup (250 mL) oat flour, $^2/_3$ cup (150 mL) natural whey protein and 6 tbsp (90 mL) vital wheat gluten. *Yield:* 3 cups (750 mL), $^1/_4$ cup (50 mL) per serving. **With Hazelnuts:** 139.1 calories, 9.6 g protein, 8.3 g fat, *6.1 g carbs*. **With Almonds:** 138.7 calories, 10.6 g protein, 7.5 g fat, *5.9 g carbs*. ***Vital Oat Ultimate Bake Mix:** (using the same formulation in main recipe): 136.5 calories, 8.1 g protein, 8.3 g fat, *6.1 g carbs*.

Soy Ultimate Bake Mix: Combine 1 cup (250 mL) ground almonds (hazelnuts, pecans or walnuts), $^2/_3$ cup (150 mL) spelt, OR all-purpose, whole wheat or whole wheat pastry flour (less carbs), $^2/_3$ cup (150 mL) soy flour and $^1/_4$ cup (50 mL) vital wheat gluten. *Yield:* $2^3/_4$ cups (675 mL), $^1/_4$ cup (50 mL) per serving. 115.4 calories, 7.7 g protein, 6.1 g fat, *8.0 g carbs*.

Helpful Hints: The ground almonds and all-purpose flour combination in Vital Ultimate Bake Mix is very similar to regular baking and often better, producing lovely, moist baked goods. With whey and soy bake mixes, replace some or all of butter in your recipes with olive oil and use whipping cream where possible, for moister baked goods. Please see Helpful Hints, page 4, for more information.

NUT-FREE ULTIMATE BAKE MIX

This works well as an alternative to the ultimate bake mixes which use ground nuts in the formulation. Use cup-for-cup instead of white, unbleached all-purpose wheat flour.

$^2/_3$ cup whole wheat pastry flour (150 mL)
$^1/_2$ cup vital wheat gluten (125 mL)
$^1/_2$ cup vanilla whey protein, OR (125 mL)
  natural whey protein powder
$^1/_2$ cup ground flax seeds, (125 mL)
$^1/_3$ cup spelt, OR all-purpose, OR (75 mL)
  whole wheat pastry flour

> **Yield:** $2^1/_2$ cups (625 mL)
> $^1/_4$ cup (50 ml) per serving
> 96.5 calories
> 10.3 g protein
> 2.2 g fat
> *7.7 g carbs*

In large bowl, combine whole wheat pastry flour, vital wheat gluten, vanilla whey protein or natural whey protein, ground flax seeds and spelt, all-purpose or whole wheat pastry flour. Mix well. Add liquid in your recipe cautiously, keeping back $^1/_4$ cup (50 mL) to $^1/_2$ cup (125 mL) liquid, and adding only as necessary, until the correct consistency is achieved.

Variation: **Nut-Free Oat Ultimate Bake Mix:** Substitute 1 cup (250 mL) oat flour, $^1/_2$ cup (125 mL) vital wheat gluten, $^1/_2$ cup (125 mL) vanilla whey protein and $^1/_2$ cup (125 mL) ground flax seeds. *Yield:* $2^1/_2$ cups (625 mL)
$^1/_4$ cup (50 ml) per serving: 99.3 calories, 10.5 g protein, 2.7 g fat, *6.3 g carbs*

Helpful Hints: This bake mix is very good in muffins and loaves, coffee cakes and many cookies, however, with more refined, delicate cakes, it may be better to switch the amounts for the whole wheat pastry flour and spelt or all-purpose flour around: (*8.4 g Carbs*). On the other hand in the main recipe, for some muffins and loaves, it is possible to use only whole wheat pastry flour and omit spelt flour or all-purpose flour. (*7.2 g Carbs*)

I tried using 1 cup (250 mL) of vanilla whey protein in this Nut-free Ultimate Bake Mix; however, baked goods were very dry. The flax seeds solve that problem nicely. Typically, this bake mix will require about the same amount of liquid as your recipe calls for, however, it is better to take the cautious route as described in the recipe instructions, just in case. Natural whey protein powder should be used in applications, where extra sweetness would be a problem.

SUNSHINE BREAD

Lovely crust on this bread and moist inside with good flavor.

$^3/_4$ cup water (175 mL)
$^1/_4$ cup whipping cream (50 mL)
$^1/_4$ cup olive oil (50 mL)
1 large egg
1 cup vital wheat gluten (250 mL)
$^2/_3$ cup whole wheat pastry flour (150 mL)
$^1/_4$ cup wheat bran (50 mL)
$^1/_4$ cup coconut, ground (50 mL)
$^1/_4$ cup sunflower seeds, ground (50 mL)
4 tsp bread machine yeast (20 mL)
1 tbsp granulated sugar (15 mL)
1 tsp salt (5 mL)
1 tsp baking powder (5 mL)

Yield: 14/16 slices
1 slice
132.8/115.5 calories
8.8/7.7 g protein
8.1/7.1 g fat
5.4/4.7 g carbs

In cereal bowl, heat water and whipping cream in microwave oven 1 minute. In bread pan, place whipping cream mixture, olive oil, egg, vital wheat gluten, whole wheat pastry flour, wheat bran, ground coconut, ground sunflower seeds, bread machine yeast, granulated sugar, salt and baking powder.

Program bread machine to Bread Rapid setting and color to medium. Remove 15 minutes before baking time is over, or when dark, golden brown in color.

Helpful Hints: This loaf cuts more easily when it is cool, however, you may not be able to wait that long! I've given two yields for convenience, as sometimes one cuts bread with less precision, especially when bread is still warm.

While kneading, etc., the bread dough will look fairly stiff after a while. The bread is lovely and moist with a good, crispy crust. Leave bread uncovered to keep the crust crisp. Cover open end with plastic wrap to prevent the open end from drying out too much. Do not leave out of the refrigerator for more than 36 hours, however, as it may spoil. Bread should freeze well for up to 1 month.

Use blender or coffee grinder in order to grind coconut and sunflower seeds.

CINNAMON RAISIN BREAD

*A lovely large, golden brown loaf with the sweet taste of cinnamon and raisins,
baked right in. Good fresh the first day and after that it makes great toast.*

$^1/_2$ cup Da Vinci® Sugar Free (125 mL)
  Cinnamon Syrup
$^1/_2$ cup water (125 mL)
3 tbsp olive oil (45 mL)
1 large egg
1 cup vital wheat gluten (250 mL)
$^3/_4$ cup whole wheat pastry flour (175 mL)
$^1/_2$ cup vanilla whey protein (125 mL)
$^1/_4$ cup oat flour (50 mL)
2 tbsp raisins, snipped in half (25 mL)
4 tsp bread machine yeast (20 mL)
1 tbsp sugar (15 ml)
2 tsp cinnamon (10 mL)
1 tsp baking powder (5 mL)
1 tsp salt (5 mL)

Yield: 16/18 slices
1 slice
87.7/78.0 calories
9.1/8.0 g protein
3.2/2.8 g fat
6.5/5.8 g carbs

In cereal bowl, heat Da Vinci® Sugar Free Cinnamon Syrup and water in
microwave oven 1 minute. In bread pan, place warmed liquid, olive oil, egg,
vital wheat gluten, whole wheat pastry flour, vanilla whey protein, oat flour,
raisins, bread machine yeast (avoid touching liquid), sugar, cinnamon, baking
powder and salt.

Program bread machine to Bread Rapid setting and color to medium. Remove
approximately 40 minutes before baking time is over, or when top of bread is
evenly dark, golden brown in color.

Variation: **Da Vinci® Alternative:** Instead use 1 cup (250 mL) water, increase
cinnamon to 1 tbsp (15 mL) and add 3 tbsp (45 mL) SPLENDA® Granular.
(*6.9 g/6.2 g Carbs*)

BLUEBERRY DESSERT CREPES

These crepes are such a good treat! Thank you, Barbara Goldstein!

Barbo's Crepes:
5 extra large eggs
$^1/_2$ cup water (125 mL)
$^1/_2$ cup whipping cream (125 mL)
$^1/_2$ cup Ultimate Bake Mix, (125 mL)
  page 67, (Whey, OR Soy UBM)
$^1/_4$ cup butter, melted (50 mL)
$^1/_4$ cup SPLENDA® Granular (50 mL)
$^1/_2$ tsp vanilla extract (2 mL)
$^1/_4$ tsp salt (1 mL)

Filling:
6 oz cream cheese, softened (180 g)
2 tbsp Da Vinci® Sugar Free Syrup, (25 mL)
  such as Pancake or Vanilla Syrup

Blueberry Sauce:
Double batch Any-Flavor Syrup, page 52
  (use Da Vinci® Sugar Free Blueberry or Huckleberry Syrup)
1 cup frozen, unsweetened blueberries (250 mL)

Yield: 12 servings
1 serving
169.5 calories
5.6 g protein
14.6 g fat
4.1 g carbs

Crepes: In blender, place eggs, water, whipping cream, Ultimate Bake Mix, page 67, butter, SPLENDA® Granular, vanilla extract and salt. Blend.

Heat 8-inch (20 cm) nonstick frying pan with a little butter. Pour $^1/_4$ cup (50 mL) batter into skillet and tilt until batter stops moving. Cook until bubbles form on top and it looks firm. Pry edges up and flip carefully. Cook few seconds longer. Repeat. **Yield:** 12 crepes. (115.8 calories, 4.1 g protein, 10.1 g fat, **2.2 g carbs**)

Blueberry Sauce: Prepare double batch of Any-Flavor Syrup, page 52. Add blueberries.

Filling and Assembly: In food processor, process cream cheese and Da Vinci® Sugar Free Syrup. Spread each crepe with a little cream cheese, roll up and place in 9 x 13-inch (23 x 33 cm) glass dish. Pour Blueberry Sauce over each crepe.

Variations: You can make Strawberry, Raspberry, Peach or Orange Dessert Crepes in the same manner, using matching flavor Da Vinci® Sugar Free Syrup.

Da Vinci® Alternative: Use Sugar Free Pancake Syrup or Maple Syrup (with vanilla extract instead of maple extract), page 172, *Splendid Low-Carbing* for filling and for Blueberry Sauce, use Da Vinci® Alternative, page 52.

FROZEN DESSERTS, POPSICLES & PUDDINGS

RASPBERRY YOGURT ICE CREAM

No eggs in this very thick and creamy protein ice cream.

$1^3/_4$ cups whipping cream (425 mL)
1 cup yogurt (250 mL)
1 cup vanilla whey protein (250 mL)
$^1/_2$ cup Da Vinci® Sugar Free (125 mL)
  Raspberry Syrup, OR flavor of choice
6 SPLENDA® packets

> **Yield:** 4 cups (1 L)
> $^1/_2$ cup (125 mL) per serving
> 220.0 calories
> 10.4 g protein
> 18.2 g fat
> ***3.4 g carbs***

In medium bowl, combine whipping cream, yogurt, vanilla whey protein, Da Vinci® Sugar Free Raspberry Syrup and SPLENDA®.

Freeze in ice cream maker, as manufacturer directs. Freeze leftovers.

Variations: **Create-a-Flavor Yogurt Ice Cream:** Use combinations of vanilla, chocolate, strawberry and raspberry whey protein with corresponding flavors of Da Vinci® Sugar Free Syrups.

Da Vinci® Alternative: Use water, 8 SPLENDA® packets and 1 tbsp (15 mL) vanilla extract. (***3.8 g Carbs***)

CHOCOLATE CREAM POPSICLES

This popsicle has a distinctly mocha flavor, however, there is no coffee in it. Great Induction or Fat Fast treat.

1 cup whipping cream (250 mL)
1 cup Da Vinci® Sugar Free (250 mL)
  Chocolate Syrup

> **Yield:** 8 popsicles
> 1 popsicle
> 90.3 calories
> 0.6 g protein
> 9.6 g fat
> *0.9 g carbs*

In large pouring jug, combine whipping cream and Da Vinci® Sugar Free Chocolate Syrup. Pour into Popsicle molds. Freeze.

Variations: **Create-a-flavor Popsicle:** Use any strong flavor Da Vinci® Sugar Free Syrup.

Da Vinci® Alternative: Use water, sugar free Kool-Aid® and sweetener to taste.

STRAWBERRY RASPBERRY POPSICLES

My sons love these. Use other fruit instead of strawberries too.

2 cups frozen strawberries, (500 mL)
  (unsweetened), slightly thawed –
  about 10 oz (300 g)
³/₄ cup Da Vinci® Sugar Free (175 mL)
  Raspberry Syrup

> **Yield:** 8 popsicles
> 1 popsicle
> 12.5 calories
> 0.1 g protein
> 0.0 g fat
> *2.5 g carbs*

In blender, combine strawberries and Da Vinci® Sugar Free Raspberry Syrup. Blend until smooth. Pour into popsicle molds.

Variations: **Peach Melba Popsicles:** Use frozen unsweetened peaches. (*4.1 g Carbs*)

Da Vinci® Alternative: Use water, 4 SPLENDA® packets and sugar free Kool-Aid® to taste. (*3.0 g Carbs*)

DOUBLE CHOCOLATE WHIRL

Rich, chocolate-y pudding with a pretty pattern on top.

1 envelope gelatin
$^1/_2$ cup Da Vinci® Sugar Free (125 mL)
  Chocolate Syrup
$^1/_4$ cup boiling water (50 mL)
2 cups whipping cream (500 mL)
$^3/_4$ cup SPLENDA® Granular (175 mL)
$^1/_3$ cup Dutch cocoa (75 mL)
$^2/_3$ cup Crème Fraiche, page 54 (150 mL)

Yield: 8 servings
1 serving
234.7 calories
3.0 g protein
22.9 g fat
5.3 g carbs

In small bowl, sprinkle gelatin over $^1/_4$ cup (50 mL) Da Vinci® Sugar Free Chocolate Syrup. Stir in boiling water until gelatin dissolves.

In blender, combine whipping cream, remaining Da Vinci® Sugar Free Chocolate Syrup, SPLENDA® Granular and cocoa. Blend well, until all cocoa is incorporated. Pour into large casserole dish and stir in gelatin mixture.

Chill 10 minutes.

Carefully drop dollops of Crème Fraiche, page 54 on top of pudding. Using sharp paring knife, swirl gently to make a pretty pattern. Refrigerate until set.

Garnish with fresh raspberries and chocolate curls, page 78, *More Splendid Low-Carbing*, if desired.

Helpful Hints: This pudding is quick to assemble. By the time lunch or supper is over, it will be ready. Serve in Champagne glasses, with extra Crème Fraiche, page 54, if desired.

EASY RHUBARB CRUMBLE

I love rhubarb (a vegetable), which is actually fairly low-carb, however, one has to add quite a bit of sweetener to make it palatable.

2.2 lb chopped, frozen rhubarb (1 kg)
$1^1/_4$ cups SPLENDA® Granular (300 mL)
1 cup Da Vinci® Sugar Free (250 mL)
  Strawberry Syrup
$^1/_2$ tsp Thickening Agent, page 57 (2 mL)
1 tbsp Crunchy Granola, page 22 (15 mL)
  per serving

Yield: 9 servings
$^1/_2$ cup (125 mL) per serving
81.8 calories
2.6 g protein
3.8 g fat
9.7 g carbs

In medium saucepan, combine rhubarb, SPLENDA® Granular and Da Vinci® Sugar Free Strawberry Syrup. Bring to boil and sprinkle in Thickening Agent, page 57, while stirring. Boil approximately 25 minutes, or until rhubarb is tender.

Allow to cool and serve with Crunchy Granola, page 22, and Crème Fraiche, page 54, or whipped cream.

Variations: Use frozen unsweetened raspberries, strawberries, peaches or blueberries instead. Reduce sweetener to taste and use a corresponding flavor of Da Vinci® Sugar Free Syrup. Reduce boiling time, as appropriate.

Da Vinci® Alternative: Use water, sugar free Kool-Aid® flavoring to taste and extra sweetener.

Lower Carb Alternative: Use 10 SPLENDA® packets. (*7.5 g Carbs*)

Helpful Hints: Frozen rhubarb can be found in some supermarkets in the frozen fruit and vegetable section. Usually it is placed with the frozen fruit, even although technically it is a vegetable. Some people have success growing their own rhubarb. The leaves of the rhubarb plant are very poisonous.

RASPBERRY JELLY

A very useful recipe during induction when something sweet is needed. It feels like you're cheating, but far from it, as this is practically a free food.

3 envelopes unflavored gelatin
$^2/_3$ cup water (150 mL)
$1^1/_3$ cups boiling water (325 mL)
$1^1/_2$ cups Da Vinci® Sugar (375 mL)
 Free Raspberry Syrup
$^1/_2$ cup ice cold water (125 mL)
$^1/_2$ tsp lemon juice (2 mL)
1 SPLENDA® packet

Yield: 4 servings
1 serving
18.7 calories
4.5 g protein
0.0 g fat
0.3 g carbs

In large bowl, combine gelatin and water, in order to soften gelatin. Stir in boiling water until gelatin dissolves completely. With wire whisk, whisk in Da Vinci® Sugar Free Raspberry Syrup, cold water, lemon juice and SPLENDA®.

Pour into 4-cup (1 L) casserole dish with lid and refrigerate until set. Garnish each serving with a dollop of Crème Fraiche, page 54, or whipped cream, if desired.

Variation: **Create-a-Flavor Jelly:** Use any flavor Da Vinci® Sugar Free Syrup or combine flavors. Omit lemon juice where it conflicts with flavor of choice.

Cream-on-top Jelly: Use $1^1/_4$ cups (300 mL) any flavor Da Vinci® Sugar Free Syrup and $^1/_4$ cup (50 mL) whipping cream. (***0.7 g Carbs***)

Da Vinci® Alternative: Replace Da Vinci® Sugar Free Raspberry Syrup with ice cold water. Use 2 packets sugar free Kool-Aid® to flavor jelly and about 6 SPLENDA® packets ($^3/_4$ cup (175 mL) SPLENDA® Granular), or to taste.
Yield: 4 servings. 1 serving: (28.0 calories, 4.5 g protein, 0.0 g fat, ***2.1 g carbs***)

PUMPKIN CUSTARD

A pleasant Thanksgiving custard. Serve with Crème Fraiche, page 54.

3 extra-large eggs
1 cup canned pumpkin, (250 mL)
  mashed
1 cup whipping cream (250 mL)
1 cup Da Vinci® Sugar (250 mL)
  Free Cinnamon Syrup
1 SPLENDA® packet
$^1/_2$ tsp ground ginger (2 mL)
$^1/_4$ tsp ground allspice (1 mL)
$^1/_8$ tsp salt (0.5 mL)

Yield: 8 servings
1 serving
130.0 calories
3.3 g protein
11.5 g fat
3.4 g carbs

In medium bowl, beat eggs with wire whisk. Stir in pumpkin, cream, Da Vinci®
Sugar Free Cinnamon Syrup, SPLENDA®, ginger, allspice and salt. Pour into
deep 9-inch (23 cm) glass baking dish.

Bake in 325°F (160°C) oven 50 minutes, or until set. Serve chilled or warm with
Crème Fraiche, page 54.

Variation: **Yellow Squash Custard:** Replace pumpkin with 1 cup (250 mL)
cooked, mashed yellow squash (rather mild-tasting and sweet for those who are
not fans of pumpkin). (***2.8 g Carbs***)

Da Vinci® Alternative: Use water, $^3/_4$ cup (175 mL) SPLENDA® Granular and
1 tsp (5 mL) cinnamon. (***5.6 g Carbs***)

MANDARIN ORANGE FROZEN YOGURT

Use a yogurt, which is not too sour. This is Daniel, my eldest son's, favorite frozen yogurt! He is not really a dessert person (except for anything made with apples), but he really enjoys this treat.

2 cups plain yogurt (500 mL)
$^1/_2$ cup SPLENDA® Granular (125 mL)
$^1/_2$ cup whipping cream (125 mL)
$^1/_4$ cup Da Vinci® Sugar Free (50 mL)
 Orange Syrup
1 cup canned mandarin oranges, (250 mL)
 in juice; drained

Yield: 5 cups (1.25 L) $^1/_2$ cup (125 mL) per serving 84.4 calories 2.5 g protein 5.5 g fat ***4.5 g carbs***

In large mixing bowl, combine yogurt, SPLENDA® Granular, whipping cream and Da Vinci® Sugar Free Orange Syrup. Stir to combine well. Stir in mandarin oranges. Freeze in ice cream maker as manufacturer directs.

Variations: **Banana Hazelnut Frozen Yogurt:** Use $^1/_2$ cup (125 mL) mashed banana and Da Vinci® Sugar Free Hazelnut or Toasted Hazelnut Syrup. Omit mandarin oranges. (***5.0 g Carbs***)

Peach Melba Frozen Yogurt: Use 1 cup (250 mL) canned unsweetened peaches in juice (drained), chopped and Da Vinci® Sugar Free Raspberry Syrup. Omit mandarin oranges. (***3.6 g Carbs***)

Strawberry Frozen Yogurt: Use 1 cup (250 mL) frozen, unsweetened strawberries, slightly thawed and mashed or sliced and Da Vinci® Sugar Free Strawberry Syrup. Omit mandarin oranges. (***3.4 g Carbs***)

Create-a-Flavor Frozen Yogurt: Use any flavor Da Vinci® Sugar Free Syrup and fruit or nut combination.

Da Vinci® Alternative: Use water and sugar free Kool-Aid® flavoring to taste and an extra $^1/_4$ cup (50 mL) SPLENDA® Granular. (***0.6 g Carbs*** increase)

PIES, CAKES & CHEESECAKES

SINGLE PIECRUST

A useful, great-tasting piecrust.

$^{3}/_{4}$ cup Whey Ultimate Bake (175 mL)
  Mix, page 67
3 oz cream cheese, softened (90 g)
1 tbsp SPLENDA® Granular (15 mL)
1 tbsp butter, softened (15 mL)
$^{1}/_{4}$ tsp baking soda (1 mL)
$^{1}/_{8}$ tsp salt (0.5 mL)

Yield: 10 servings	
1 serving	
76.4 calories	
3.9 g protein	
5.5 g fat	
2.8 g carbs	

In food processor or in bowl with electric mixer, process Ultimate Bake Mix, page 67, cream cheese, SPLENDA® Granular, butter, baking soda and salt, until mixed.

At this point it is best to wrap dough in wax paper or plastic wrap and chill for a few hours, or alternatively place it in the freezer for 20 minutes.

Roll dough out between two large sheets of wax paper. Pick up bottom sheet, including piecrust and gently invert into 9-inch (23 cm) glass pie dish. Patch where necessary.

Make an attractive edging. Prick crust all over. Bake in 350°F (180°C) oven 15 minutes, or until golden brown.

Variation: **Single Oat Piecrust:** Use Nut-Free Oat Ultimate Bake Mix, page 68, or Vital Oat Ultimate Bake Mix or Oat Ultimate Bake Mix, page 67. (***2.3 g Carbs***).

RASPBERRY CUSTARD PIE

A recipe to take ordinary custard pie up a notch in looks and taste. The idea for this pie came from Jeanne Lobsinger of Vernon, British Columbia.

Single Piecrust, page 79
Filling:
3 extra-large eggs
Condensed Milk,* page 56
$^1/_2$ cup boiling water (125 mL)
$^1/_2$ cup Da Vinci® Sugar Free (125 mL)
  French Vanilla Syrup
$^1/_4$ tsp salt (1 mL)
1 cup frozen raspberries, (250 mL)
  (unsweetened)

Yield: 10 servings
1 serving
217.6 calories
8.6 g protein
17.1 g fat
7.5 g carbs

Single Piecrust: Follow directions on page 79. Make sure crust comes up sides of pie dish; make an attractive edging. Bake only 5 minutes in 350°F (180°F) oven.

Filling: In large mixing bowl, beat eggs. Add Condensed Milk, page 56, boiling water, Da Vinci® Sugar Free French Vanilla Syrup and salt. Whisk well. Gently stir in raspberries. Pour carefully over prepared pastry shell. Evenly distribute raspberries. Carefully place in 400°F (200°C) oven. Cover with large foil tent (sides folded over for support on oven rack – foil must not touch custard) and bake 10 minutes. Reduce temperature to 350°F (180°C) and continue baking 40 minutes, or until custard has puffed up and looks softly set. Refrigerate.

Variations: **Strawberry Custard Pie:** Use sliced, frozen unsweetened strawberries. (*8.6 g Carbs*)

Blueberry Custard Pie: Use frozen unsweetened blueberries. (*8.9 g Carbs*)

Peach Custard Pie: Use frozen or canned, unsweetened peaches, chopped. (*8.8 g Carbs*)

Da Vinci® Alternative: Use water, vanilla extract and also $^1/_4$ cup (50 mL) SPLENDA® Granular. (*8.1 g Carbs*)

Helpful Hints: *Thickening Agent in Condensed Milk, page 56, is not necessary. Instead of Da Vinci® Sugar Free French Vanilla Syrup, substitute any flavor that would be appropriate as well. If using Single Oat Piecrust, page 79, subtract 0.5 g carbohydrate per serving.

APPLE PIE ALMONDINE

Few apples, but just enough to give that great apple pie taste!

Crust:
1 cup ground almonds (250 mL)
1 SPLENDA® packet
1 egg white
Filling:
2 cups diced, peeled apples (500 mL)
$^1/_2$ cup SPLENDA® Granular (125 mL)
$^1/_4$ cup ground almonds (50 mL)
3 tbsp butter, diced (45 mL)
2 tbsp raisins, snipped (25 mL)
2 tsp lemon juice (10 mL)
$^1/_2$ tsp vanilla extract (2 mL)
$^1/_2$ tsp cinnamon (2 mL)
$1^2/_3$ cups Crème Fraiche, page 54 (400 mL)
1 tbsp ground almonds, toasted* (15 mL)

Yield: 10 servings
1 serving
205.5 calories
4.2 g protein
17.0 g fat
9.2 g carbs

Crust: In small bowl, combine ground almonds, SPLENDA® and egg white. Spread in bottom of 9-inch (23 cm) greased glass baking dish. Cover with plastic wrap and press out evenly; remove wrap. Bake in 350°F (180°C) oven 5 minutes.

Filling: In large bowl, stir together apples, SPLENDA® Granular, ground almonds, butter, raisins, lemon juice, vanilla extract and cinnamon. Fill piecrust. Bake in 350°F (180°C) oven 30 minutes. After 15 minutes, place sheet of aluminum foil over top. Remove from oven and allow to cool completely. Cover with Crème Fraiche, page 54, and sprinkle with toasted, ground almonds. Garnish with sliced almonds around perimeter and raw, whole almonds in center, if desired.

Variations: **Peach Pie Almondine:** Use canned, unsweetened peaches in juice, drained, or fresh peaches, chopped. (***8.8 g Carbs***)

Pear Pie Almondine: Use canned, unsweetened pears in juice, drained, or fresh pears, chopped. (***9.1 g Carbs***)

Helpful Hint: *In nonstick skillet, toast ground almonds over medium heat until golden.

CARAMEL PIE

Don't say I didn't warn everyone! One slice of the rich taste of caramel condensed milk poured over a piecrust will not be enough.

Crust:
1 cup ground almonds (250 mL)
1 SPLENDA® packet
1 egg white, fork beaten
Filling:
$^1/_4$ cup whipping cream (50 mL)
1 envelope gelatin
$^2/_3$ cup Da Vinci® Sugar Free (150 mL)
  Caramel Syrup
$^2/_3$ cup butter, semi-melted (150 mL)
$^2/_3$ cup vanilla whey protein (150 mL)
$^2/_3$ cup whole milk powder, OR (150 mL)
  skim milk powder
2 tbsp water (25 mL)
3 SPLENDA® packets, OR to taste
$^1/_2$ oz unsweetened baking chocolate, grated (15 g)
  (optional)

Yield: 10 servings
1 serving
264.3 calories
10.1 g protein
23.0 g fat
5.1 g carbs

Crust: In small bowl, combine ground almonds, SPLENDA® and egg white. Place in bottom of 9-inch (23 cm) greased glass baking dish. Cover with plastic wrap; press crust out. Remove wrap. Bake in 350°F (180°C) oven 10 minutes. Cover with foil and bake 5 to 7 more minutes.

Filling: In cereal bowl, combine whipping cream and gelatin. Set aside. In blender, combine Da Vinci® Sugar Free Caramel Syrup, butter, vanilla whey protein, whole milk powder, water and SPLENDA®. Blend. Heat cream mixture in microwave oven 75 seconds to dissolve gelatin. Add to blender and blend condensed milk mixture until smooth. Pour mixture over crust. Cover pie dish with plastic wrap, but do not touch surface of pie (it will stick). When pie has set, sprinkle with grated unsweetened chocolate, if desired, for garnish.

Variations: Caramel Pudding: Simply leave out the crust.
Yield: 10 servings. (193.3 calories, 7.4 g protein, 16.8 g fat, *4.1 g carbs*)

Create-a-Flavor Pie – Use Da Vinci® Sugar Free Dulce De Leche Syrup or chocolate whey protein and Da Vinci® Sugar Free Chocolate Syrup, etc.

Da Vinci® Alternative: Use caramel or butterscotch extract to taste, water and extra sweetener, or use sugar free chocolate syrup and chocolate extract.

MINI HOT CHOCOLATE CAKES

An elegant dessert you can serve with great delight after a light dinner. My husband and son, Jonathan, rave about this dessert – even just the memory of enjoying it, brings rave reviews from them!

5 oz sugar free chocolate, (150 g)
  (sweetened with maltitol usually)
2 tbsp unsalted butter (25 mL)
1 SPLENDA® packet
2 extra-large eggs, separated
$^1/_4$ tsp vanilla extract (1 mL)
3 tbsp Crème Fraiche, page 54 (45 mL)
6 raspberries
6 tbsp Chocolate Drizzle, (90 mL)
  page 84, (optional)

Yield: 3 servings
1 serving
305.4 calories
7.1 g protein
30.7 g fat
3.5 g carbs

In double boiler over hot, boiling water, melt chocolate and butter together, and stir until smooth. Remove from heat and whisk in SPLENDA® and egg yolks.

In food processor, or in bowl with electric mixer, beat egg whites and vanilla extract until stiff. Fold $^1/_3$ of beaten egg whites into chocolate mixture, and then fold remaining egg whites into chocolate batter.

Spray 3 custard cups or ramekins with nonstick cooking spray. Divide batter evenly between them. Place on baking sheet and bake in 400°F (200°C) oven 12 to 15 minutes. They will look and feel slightly set in the center (no molten chocolate visible).

Allow to stand 2 minutes before inverting onto pretty dessert plates. Garnish each cake with Crème Fraiche, page 54, and 2 raspberries. Pour Chocolate Drizzle, page 84, if using, over each cake.

Helpful Hints: The chocolate batter may be assembled earlier in the day, poured into ramekins, and baked just before serving. This is an intensely chocolate-y dessert for chocolate lovers. Recipe may be doubled to serve 6.

It works out cheaper for me to buy sugar free chocolate chips instead of chocolate bars, and then determine the amount needed by weighing them on my electronic kitchen scale.

HAZELNUT CHOCOLATE BUNDT CAKE

Lovely cake without flour.

2$\frac{1}{2}$ oz sugar free chocolate, (45 g)
  (sweetened with maltitol usually)
$\frac{1}{3}$ cup butter (75 mL)
6 extra-large eggs, separated
$\frac{1}{4}$ tsp lemon juice (1 mL)
1 cup SPLENDA® Granular (250 mL)
1$\frac{2}{3}$ cups ground hazelnuts (400 mL)
1 cup Crème Fraiche, page 54 (250 mL)
few raspberries for garnish, (optional)
Chocolate Drizzle:
$\frac{1}{4}$ cup sugar free chocolate chips, (50 mL)
  (sweetened with maltitol usually)
1 tbsp unsalted butter (15 mL)
1 tbsp whipping cream (15 mL)

Yield: 16 servings
1 serving
216.4 calories
4.9 g protein
20.8 g fat
3.9 g carbs

Line 10-inch (4 L) bundt pan with wax paper (leaving edges high). Spray liberally with nonstick cooking spray. Set aside.

In double boiler, melt chocolate and butter. In food processor, process egg whites and lemon juice until stiff. In small bowl, whisk egg yolks and SPLENDA® Granular together until smooth. Whisk in chocolate mixture.

Fold ground hazelnuts and chocolate mixture into beaten egg whites. Pour batter into prepared pan. Bake in 350°F (180°C) oven 30 minutes, or until cake tester comes out clean. Invert bundt pan on wire rack and carefully remove paper.

Chocolate Drizzle: In double boiler, melt chocolate chips and butter. Stir in whipping cream.

Spread cooled cake with Crème Fraiche, page 54, add a few fresh raspberries, if desired, and drizzle with chocolate.

Variation: **Almond Chocolate Bundt Cake:** Use ground almonds instead of ground hazelnuts.

Helpful Hints: Ground hazelnuts are typically quite pricey compared to ground almonds. It may be cheaper to grind your own, or simply use ground almonds instead.

TRIPLE CHOCOLATE CUPCAKES

Decadent-tasting, large cupcakes - indistinguishable from the high-carb variety.

2 cups Whey Ultimate Bake (500 mL)
  Mix,* page 67 (using ground hazelnuts)
1³/₄ cups SPLENDA® Granular (425 mL)
³/₄ cup Dutch cocoa (175 mL)
2 tsp baking powder (10 mL)
1 tsp baking soda (5 mL)
¹/₈ tsp salt (0.5 mL)
2 eggs
³/₄ cup Da Vinci® Sugar Free (175 mL)
  Chocolate Syrup
¹/₂ cup sour cream (125 mL)
7 tbsp olive oil (105 mL)
1 cup sugar free chocolate chips, (sweetened) (250 mL)
Chocolate Fudge Frosting, page 95

Yield: 16 cupcakes
1 cupcake
204.9 calories
7.8 g protein
15.8 g fat
9.0 g carbs

In large bowl, combine Whey Ultimate Bake Mix, page 67, SPLENDA® Granular, cocoa, baking powder, baking soda and salt. In large mixing bowl, beat eggs. Add Da Vinci® Sugar Free Chocolate Syrup, sour cream and olive oil. Add dry ingredients gradually, while beating. Beat on medium speed about 2 minutes. Stir in chocolate chips.

Line 2 muffin tins with 16 cupcake liners. Fill each about ²/₃ full with cake batter. Bake in 350°F (180°C) oven 18 to 20 minutes, or until cake tester comes out clean. Remove cupcakes and cool on wire rack. Spread cupcakes with Chocolate Fudge Frosting, page 95. Garnish each chocolate cupcake with a little SPLENDA® -sweetened coconut, if desired.

Chocolate Fudge Frosting: Prepare Chocolate Fudge Frosting, page 95.

Variation: **Da Vinci® Alternative:** Use 2 tsp (10 mL) chocolate extract and water. Add extra ¹/₄ cup (50 mL) SPLENDA® Granular, if desired. (***9.4 g Carbs***)

Helpful Hints: Instead of Chocolate Fudge Frosting, page 95, you could use Chocolate Drizzle, page 84: (***7.8 g Carbs***). I used all-purpose flour instead of spelt flour in the Whey Ultimate Bake Mix, page 67, formulation. If chocolate chips are unavailable, chop sugar free chocolate (such as Ross® bars) in food processor (use pulse button). Alternatively, use 1 cup (250 mL) chopped, blanched hazelnuts. (***9.4 g Carbs***) These delicious cupcakes are best eaten within 24 hours. *****Vital Ultimate Bake Mix,** page 67, would probably extend the life of these cupcakes as the bake mix produces a moister baked product. (***9.0 g Carbs***)

MINI CHEESE CUPCAKES

Lovely for parties, to add to an array of desserts – looks pretty.

16 oz regular cream cheese, (500 g)
  softened
$^1/_2$ cup SPLENDA® Granular (125 mL)
$^1/_4$ cup sour cream (50 mL)
$^1/_4$ cup Da Vinci® Sugar Free (50 mL)
  Strawberry Syrup, OR any flavor
2 eggs
$^3/_4$ cup Crème Fraiche, page 54 (175 mL)

Yield: 12 servings
1 serving
176.3 calories
5.2 g protein
16.0 g fat
3.2 g carbs

In food processor with sharp blade or electric mixer, process softened cream cheese and SPLENDA® Granular until smooth. Add sour cream and Da Vinci® Sugar Free Strawberry Syrup, or flavor of choice; process. Add eggs and process just until eggs are incorporated. Line one muffin tin with 12 cupcake liners. Fill halfway with cheesecake batter.

Bake in 350°F (180°C) oven 30 to 40 minutes. Allow to cool half an hour. Garnish each mini cheese cupcake with 1 tbsp (15 mL) Crème Fraiche, page 54. Refrigerate until cold.

Variation: **Lemon Curd Cheese Cupcakes:** Increase SPLENDA® Granular to $^3/_4$ cup (175 mL), and add 3 tbsp (45 mL) whipping cream, 2 tsp (10 mL) grated lemon peel, and 2 tsp (10 mL) lemon juice. Omit Da Vinci® Sugar Free Syrup and Crème Fraiche, page 54.

Garnish cooled cupcakes with a little less than a tablespoon (15 mL) Lemon Curd, page 60, just before serving. (*4.0 g Carbs*)

Helpful Hints: If desired, sprinkle some ground almonds in bottom of each cupcake liner, to serve as a simple no-fuss crust. Pour cheesecake batter carefully over top with a spoon.

MARBLE-FROSTED CHOCOLATE CHEESECAKE

Frosting on this lower calorie cheesecake looks beautiful and tastes incredible.

2 cups 2% cottage cheese (500 mL)
8 oz regular cream cheese, (250 g)
  softened
1 cup sour cream (250 mL)
1 cup SPLENDA® Granular (250 mL)
2 eggs
$^1/_2$ cup chocolate whey protein (125 mL)
$^1/_4$ cup Da Vinci® Sugar Free (50 mL)
  Chocolate Syrup
3 tbsp Dutch cocoa (45 mL)

Topping:
$^2/_3$ cup Condensed Milk, page 56 (150 mL)
1 oz unsweetened baking chocolate, melted (30 g)

Yield: 12 servings
1 serving
235.1 calories
13.7 g protein
16.8 g fat
7.6 g carbs

In food processor with sharp blade, blender or in bowl with electric mixer, process cottage cheese until smooth. Add cream cheese, sour cream, SPLENDA® Granular and eggs; process. Add chocolate whey protein, Da Vinci® Sugar Free Chocolate Syrup and cocoa; process. Pour in 9-inch (23 cm) springform pan or glass pie dish. Bake in 350°F (180°C) oven 45 minutes.

Topping: In small bowl, combine Condensed Milk (except for 2 tbsp (25 mL), page 56, and chocolate. Spread frosting over middle of cooled cheesecake, which will have sunk in the middle, leaving a beautiful edge all around the perimeter. With a teaspoon drop blobs of remaining Condensed Milk over chocolate frosting. Swirl gently at a shallow depth with a sharp, paring knife.

Variations: **Marble-Frosted Strawberry Cheesecake:** Use strawberry whey protein and Da Vinci® Sugar Free Strawberry Syrup. Omit cocoa. Add 2 tbsp (25 mL) vital wheat gluten. (***7.7 g Carbs***)

Marble-Frosted Raspberry Cheesecake: Use raspberry whey protein and Da Vinci® Sugar Free Raspberry Syrup. Omit cocoa. Add 2 tbsp (25 mL) vital wheat gluten. (***7.7 g Carbs***)

Marble-Frosted Vanilla Cheesecake: Use vanilla whey protein and Da Vinci® Sugar Free French Vanilla or Vanilla Syrup. Omit cocoa. Add 2 tbsp (15 mL) vital wheat gluten. (***7.7 g Carbs***)

Da Vinci® Alternative: Omit syrup. Add an extra tablespoon (15 mL) Dutch cocoa and extra sweetener to taste. This will be a firmer cheesecake.

B-52 CHEESECAKE

This is a fabulous cheesecake. Use any flavor Da Vinci® Syrup to change this cheesecake into an entirely different cheesecake. B-52 is a mixture of Kahlua, Amaretto and Irish Cream in equal quantities.

Crust:
1 cup ground almonds (250 mL)
1 SPLENDA® packet
1 egg white

Filling:
24 oz regular, OR light cream (750 g) cheese, softened
1¹/₂ cups SPLENDA® Granular (375 mL)
¹/₃ cup Da Vinci® Sugar Free B-52 Syrup (75 mL)
1 tbsp spelt flour (15 mL)
¹/₂ tsp vanilla extract (2 mL)
3 eggs

Topping:
1 cup sour cream (250 mL)
3 tbsp SPLENDA® Granular (45 mL)
1 tbsp Da Vinci® Sugar Free B-52 Syrup (15 mL)
¹/₄ tsp vanilla extract (1 mL)
1 cup fresh raspberries (250 mL)

> *Yield:* 12/16 servings
> 1 serving
> 276.7/207.5 calories
> 9.9 g/7.4 g protein
> 22.5 g/16.9 g fat
> ***8.8 g/6.6 g carbs***

Crust: In small bowl, combine ground almonds, SPLENDA® and egg white. Spread in 9-inch (23 cm) springform pan. Cover with plastic wrap. Press crust out evenly; remove wrap. Bake in 350°F (180°C) oven 10 minutes. Cover with foil and bake 5 more minutes.

Filling: In food processor with sharp blade, blender or in bowl with electric mixer, process cream cheese until smooth. Add SPLENDA® Granular, Da Vinci® Sugar Free B-52 Syrup, spelt flour and vanilla extract; process. Add eggs, one at a time and process just until incorporated. Pour mixture over prepared crust. Bake in 350°F (180°C) oven 40 minutes, or until firmly set around perimeter and softly set in center. Allow to cool. Refrigerate.

Topping: In small bowl, combine sour cream, SPLENDA® Granular, Da Vinci® Sugar Free B-52 Syrup and vanilla extract. Spread over chilled cheesecake. Garnish with raspberries.

Variation: Da Vinci® Alternative: Use whipping cream and increase flavored extract of choice, to taste. (***9.0 g/6.7 g Carbs***)

CONFECTIONS & FROSTINGS

CHOCOLATE PEANUT BUTTER CANDY

This yummy confection is going to very strongly remind you of peanut butter cups! My family and especially Jonathan loved it. He keeps asking me to make it. Ian said, "This recipe alone is worth the price of the book!" – and this from someone who is not a fan of peanut butter!

$^1/_4$ cup unsalted butter (50 mL)
$^1/_4$ cup coconut oil (50 mL)
1 oz unsweetened chocolate, (30 g)
9 SPLENDA® packets
$^1/_4$ cup vanilla whey protein (50 mL)
$^1/_4$ cup whole milk powder (50 mL)
$^1/_4$ cup peanut butter,* (50 mL)
   sugar free (can contain salt)
1 tbsp whipping cream (15 mL)

Yield: 36 pieces
1 piece
47.4 calories
1.1 g protein
4.5 g fat
1.0 g carbs

In double boiler, melt butter, coconut oil and chocolate. In food processor with sharp blade, blender or in bowl with electric mixer, pour melted chocolate mixture. Add SPLENDA®, vanilla whey protein, milk powder, peanut butter and whipping cream. Process. Pour into 8-inch (20 cm) square glass baking dish. Freeze very solid. This candy needs no thawing; using a knife, pieces break easily.

Variation: **Chocolate Almond Butter Candy:** Use almond butter and a pinch of salt.

Helpful Hints: *If peanut butter is unsalted, add a pinch of salt to the recipe. 1 cup (250 mL) SPLENDA® Granular may be used instead of SPLENDA® packets. (*1.5 g Carbs*).

The above analysis is a rough estimate, as the pieces that break are not uniform in size. Do not be worried by the texture of the pre-frozen product – it tastes wonderful and different once completely frozen. Double the recipe – you'll be glad you did!

CREAMY TOFFEE

Excellent treat – smooth and creamy, chewy toffee.

9 oz regular cream cheese, (280 g)
  softened
$^1/_2$ cup unsalted butter (125 mL)
3 oz unsweetened chocolate, (90 g)
1 oz cocoa butter (30 g)
$1^1/_2$ cups chocolate whey protein (375 mL)
  OR vanilla whey protein
1 cup SPLENDA® Granular (250 mL)
1 cup whole milk powder* (250 mL)
4 SPLENDA® packets

> *Yield:* 98 pieces (14 x 7)
> 1 piece
> 35.8 calories
> 1.7 g protein
> 2.9 g fat
> *1.1 g carbs*

In food processor with sharp blade, blender or in bowl with electric mixer, process cream cheese until smooth.

Over medium heat in double boiler, melt butter, chocolate and cocoa butter. Add to cream cheese, along with chocolate or vanilla whey protein, SPLENDA® Granular, whole milk powder and SPLENDA®. Process slowly and then at high speed, until smooth. Press into 9 x 13-inch (23 x 33 cm) glass baking dish. Refrigerate or freeze. Cut into pieces, before toffee freezes too hard, if desired. Then store in covered container in freezer or refrigerator.

Variation: **Truffles:** Using a melon baller for approximate size, roll little balls of freshly made toffee in Splenda-sweetened coconut, Hot Chocolate Drink Mix, *Splendid Low-Carbing*, page 15, grated sugar free chocolate or dip in Dipping Chocolate, *Splendid Low-Carbing*, page 175. Place truffles in pretty colorful candy paper cups. Great for Christmas time or Valentine's Day or for a special treat anytime.

Helpful Hints: *Skim milk powder may be used instead; blend finely in blender.

Cut into squares and either freeze or refrigerate, according to preference. The frozen product takes a couple of minutes at room temperature to thaw. Use the freezer compartment of the refrigerator, which is not quite as cold as a large freezer.

WHITE CHOCOLATE PROTEIN BARS

Delicious, sweet, chewy protein bars to carry in your purse.

1 oz cocoa butter (30 g)
1 cup vanilla whey protein (250 mL)
$^1/_4$ cup whole milk powder (50 mL)
5 SPLENDA® packets
2 tbsp Da Vinci® Sugar Free (25 mL)
  White Chocolate Syrup
2 tbsp butter, melted (25 mL)
2 tbsp diced almonds, divided (25 mL)

Yield: 4/5/6 protein bars
1 protein bar
238.6/190.9/159.1 calories
18.8/15.1/12.6 g protein
16.1/12.9/10.7 g fat
5.6/4.4/3.7 g carbs

In covered cereal bowl, melt cocoa butter in microwave oven (about 4 minutes).

In medium bowl, combine vanilla whey protein, whole milk powder and SPLENDA®. Stir in Da Vinci® Sugar Free White Chocolate Syrup and butter. Stir in melted cocoa butter. Turn out on cutting board. Knead well.

Sprinkle half almonds on cutting board. Form a rectangle with mixture over top of almonds, that is 6 x 5-inches (15 x 12 cm) and cut into 6 bars. For 5 and 4 bars, form a rectangle 5 x 5-inches (12 x 12 cm) and 4 x 5-inches (10 x 12 cm) respectively.

Basically, each bar is about 1-inch (2.5 cm) in diameter and 5 inches (12 cm) long. The bars will be thicker for the smaller yield. Sprinkle remaining almonds over top and press into top surface. Refrigerate. Protein Bars should last at room temperature, at least a few days, if required.

Helpful Hint: Do be careful with hot cocoa butter!

DOUBLE CHOCOLATE PROTEIN BARS

So easy to make and have ready in minutes! Tastes great too!

1 oz unsweetened chocolate (30 g)
³/₄ cup chocolate whey protein (175 mL)
3 tbsp whole milk powder (45 mL)
4 SPLENDA® packets
3 tbsp whipping cream (45 mL)
2 tbsp unsalted butter, (25 mL)
  melted
3 tbsp diced almonds (45 mL)

Yield: 3/4/5 protein bars
1 protein bar
330.9/248.2/198.5 calories
18.3/13.8/11.0 g protein
25.6/19.2/15.4 g fat
8.7/6.5/5.2 g carbs

In cereal bowl, microwave chocolate 2 minutes. In another small bowl, combine chocolate whey protein, whole milk powder, SPLENDA®, whipping cream and butter. Stir in chocolate. Use hands to knead stiff mixture.

Sprinkle half diced almonds on dinner plate. Pat mixture out over top of almonds into 5-inch (12 cm) square and divide in 5 equal parts {1-inch (2.5 cm) thick} longitudinally.

If making the smaller number of bars, pat mixture into a 3 x 5-inch (8 x 12 cm) or a 4 x 5-inch (10 x 12 cm) rectangle.

Press the remaining almonds over surface of protein bars. Freeze 10 minutes, or until firm, and refrigerate.

Variations: **Strawberry or Raspberry Chocolate Protein Bars:** Substitute strawberry or raspberry whey protein for the chocolate whey protein. Add a little strawberry or raspberry extract, if desired, for a stronger flavor.

VANILLA WHEY FROSTING

Condensed milk-like. I'll admit I enjoy the Chocolate Vanilla Whey frosting to snack on when chocolate cravings hit me. The next day, after refrigerating, it becomes more toffee-like.

$^3/_4$ cup vanilla whey protein (175 mL)
3 tbsp whole, OR skim milk (45 mL)
  powder*
6 SPLENDA® packets
$^1/_4$ cup Da Vinci® Sugar Free (50 mL)
  French Vanilla or Vanilla Syrup
3 tbsp butter, at room temp. (45 mL)

Yield: 12/16 servings
1 serving
56.1/42.4 calories
4.6 g/3.4 g protein
3.6 g/2.7 g fat
1.5 g/1.1 g carbs

In medium bowl, combine vanilla whey protein, whole or skim milk powder and SPLENDA®. With metal spoon, stir in Da Vinci® Sugar Free French Vanilla or Vanilla Syrup, until mixture is as smooth as possible. Work in softened butter, until well combined.

Variations: **Da Vinci® Alternative:** Use $3^1/_2$ tbsp (52 mL) water , 1 tsp (5 mL) vanilla extract and an extra SPLENDA® packet, or to taste.

Create-a-Flavor Whey Frosting: Use any flavor whey protein with Da Vinci® Sugar Free Syrup of choice. For example, use vanilla whey protein with Da Vinci® Sugar Free White Chocolate Syrup for a White Chocolate Whey Frosting.

Chocolate Vanilla Whey Frosting: Use vanilla whey protein, Da Vinci® Sugar Free Chocolate Syrup, 1 tbsp (15 mL) whole milk powder and 2 tbsp Dutch cocoa. (***1.1 g/0.8 g Carbs***)

Helpful Hints: *If using coarsely ground skim milk powder, blend finely in blender first and then measure. If the consistency of the frosting is too soft, refrigerate until firmer.

93

HAZELNUT CHOCOLATE FROSTING

Very similar to a fabulous, chocolate hazelnut spread called Nutella®.

1 cup Hot Chocolate Drink* (250 mL)
  Mix, page 15, *Splendid Low-Carbing*
$^1/_2$ cup Crème Fraiche, page 54 (125 mL)
4 tbsp Da Vinci® Sugar Free (50 mL)
  Hazelnut Syrup
2 SPLENDA® packets, (optional)

Yield: 12/16 servings
1 serving
42.1/31.6 calories
1.4/1.0 g protein
2.8/2.1 g fat
3.1/2.3 g carbs

In medium bowl, whisk together Hot Chocolate Drink Mix, page 15, *Splendid Low-Carbing*, Crème Fraiche, page 54, and SPLENDA®, if using. Add Da Vinci® Sugar Free Hazelnut Syrup, gradually adding the last tablespoon (15 mL) to get the correct consistency.

Variations: **Raspberry Chocolate Frosting:** Use Da Vinci® Sugar Free Raspberry Syrup.

Create-a-flavor Chocolate Frosting: Use your own flavor of Da Vinci® Sugar Free Syrup.

Helpful Hints: This makes enough delicious frosting for a double layer cake or a Bundt cake or a 9 x 13-inch (23 x 33 cm) cake. *It is imperative to use Dutch cocoa (available in health food stores or online) in the Hot Chocolate Drink Mix, page 15, *Splendid* Low-Carbing, for this recipe to taste best. For an even sweeter frosting, add the extra sweetener.

This goes well with low-carb waffles, along with serving other toppings, such as blueberry sauce, fresh strawberries, Crème Fraiche, page 54, and Maple Syrup, page 172, *Splendid Low-Carbing*. See Cream Cheese Bran Waffles, page 20.

CHOCOLATE FUDGE FROSTING

Deliciously rich! This frosting can easily be doubled for a double-layer cake. It produces enough to cover an 8-inch (20 cm) square surface, as in over brownies.

$^1/_3$ cup Crème Fraiche, page 54 (75 mL)
5 SPLENDA® packets
2 tbsp whole or skim milk (25 mL)
  powder*
1 oz baking chocolate, (30 g)
  (unsweetened)

> **Yield:** 16/25/36 servings
> 1 serving
> 24.2/15.5/10.7 calories
> 0.5/0.3/0.2 g protein
> 2.1/1.3/0.9 g fat
> *1.1/0.7/0.5 g carbs*

In small bowl, combine Crème Fraiche, page 54, SPLENDA® and whole milk powder. Stir well.

In cereal bowl, microwave chocolate 2 minutes to melt. Stir into Crème Fraiche mixture until well combined. Spread over brownies immediately.

Variation: **Creamy Chocolate Frosting:** For a mousse-like frosting, stir in an extra $^2/_3$ cup (150 mL) Crème Fraiche, page 54. Enough to frost a double-layered cake. Or, one could slice brownies in half, frost, replace top half and frost again. *Yield:* 12/16/25 servings. (*3.3 g/2.5 g/1.6 g/ Carbs*)

Helpful Hints: *Skim milk powder should be blended in blender until fine, unless it is already finely ground.

One may use $^3/_4$ cup (175 mL) SPLENDA® Granular instead of the packets, if desired, for approximately 0.5 g carb increase. If desired, increase sweetness to 6 SPLENDA® packets, however, I found 5 packets made the frosting sweet enough for my taste.

RASPBERRY CHOCOLATE FUDGE

Melted, sweetened chocolate will pool on top and harden in refrigerator – very tasty fudge! See lower carb alternative below.

2 cups SPLENDA® Granular* (500 mL)
³/₄ cup whole OR skim milk (175 mL)
  powder (blend skim milk powder)
6 tbsp vanilla whey protein, OR (90 mL)
  chocolate whey protein
6 tbsp unsalted butter, melted (90 mL)
2 tbsp Da Vinci® Sugar Free (25 mL)
  Raspberry Syrup
2 oz unsweetened chocolate, melted (60 g)

Yield: 36 pieces
1 piece
46.8 calories
1.6 g protein
3.5 g fat
2.6 g carbs

In medium bowl, combine SPLENDA® Granular, whole or skim milk powder and vanilla whey protein or chocolate whey protein. With a wooden spoon, stir in butter and Da Vinci® Sugar Free Raspberry Syrup, until as smooth as possible. In cereal bowl, microwave 2 chocolate squares 2 minutes, until melted. Stir chocolate into mixture as best possible.

Place in 8-inch (20 cm) square glass baking dish and press out with back of spoon. Refrigerate.

Variations: **Create-a-Flavor Chocolate Fudge:** Use your choice of flavor for Da Vinci® Sugar Free Syrup.

Lower Carb Alternative: *Use 16 SPLENDA® packets instead of SPLENDA® Granular. (*1.8 g Carbs*)

Da Vinci® Alternative: Instead, use 2 tbsp (25 mL) water, 1 tsp (5 mL) vanilla extract and 1 SPLENDA® packet. (*2.7 g Carbs/1.9 g Carbs*) The second value in parentheses is the lower carb alternative.

CARAMEL PECAN FUDGE

After thawing slightly, this sweet, caramel-flavored confection tastes quite fudge-like.

2 cups Confectioner's Sugar (500 mL)
  Substitute, page 53
$^1/_4$ cup Da Vinci® Sugar Free (50 mL)
  Caramel Syrup
$^1/_4$ cup whipping cream (50 mL)
2 tbsp butter, melted (25 mL)
2 oz cocoa butter, melted (60 g)
$^1/_2$ cup chopped pecans (125 mL)

Yield: 72 pieces
1 piece
25.0 calories
0.7 g protein
2.1 g fat
0.9 g carbs

In large mixing bowl, mix Confectioner's Sugar Substitute, page 53, Da Vinci® Sugar Free Caramel Syrup, whipping cream and butter, until well combined. Stir in melted cocoa butter (microwave in covered cereal bowl approximately 4 minutes), until smooth. Stir in pecans. Turn out into 8-inch (20 cm) square glass baking dish. Cover with plastic wrap and press out evenly. Keep in freezer. Allow to thaw 8 to 10 minutes, before cutting a small piece (see Helpful Hint).

Variations: **White Chocolate Pecan Fudge:** Use Da Vinci® Sugar Free White Chocolate Syrup instead of the caramel flavor. (*0.9 g Carbs*)

Milk Chocolate Almond Fudge: Follow main recipe, but omit 1 oz (30 g) cocoa butter. Substitute 1 oz (30 g) cocoa butter and 1 oz (30 g) unsweetened chocolate (melt in microwave oven 2 minutes and stir to melt remaining cocoa butter), $^1/_2$ cup (125 mL) whole raw almonds, $^1/_4$ cup (50 mL) Da Vinci® Sugar Free Chocolate Syrup instead of the caramel flavor and 2 SPLENDA® packets. Freeze until hard, then refrigerate, or keep frozen. (*1.0 g Carbs*)

Dark Chocolate Almond Fudge: For a darker chocolate, follow the Milk Chocolate Almond Fudge recipe and omit cocoa butter altogether. Substitute 2 oz (60 g) unsweetened chocolate. Freeze until hard, then refrigerate, or keep frozen. (*1.1 g Carbs*)

Create-a-Flavor Pecan Fudge: Use any other appropriate Da Vinci® Sugar Free Syrup.

Da Vinci® Alternative: Use water and 2 tsp (10 mL) caramel, butterscotch, chocolate extract or any other extract. Add extra sweetener, if necessary.

Helpful Hint: Nuke confection in glass dish approximately 7 to 15 seconds, depending on how much is left, for easy removal.

CHOCOLATE NUGGETS

Two more fudge-like confections – quite solid and firm. This is a dark chocolate as opposed to a milk chocolate flavor. For more of a milk chocolate flavor, use half cocoa butter and half unsweetened chocolate.

3 oz regular cream cheese, (90 g)
  softened
2 oz unsweetened chocolate (60 g)
2 cups Confectioner's Sugar, (500 mL)
  Substitute, page 53
$^1/_4$ cup SPLENDA® Granular (50 mL)
$1^1/_2$ tbsp whipping cream (22 mL)
$^1/_4$ tsp vanilla extract (1 mL)
$^3/_4$ cup pecan halves (175 mL)

Yield: 72 nuggets
1 nugget
18.1 calories
0.8 g protein
1.2 g fat
1.1 g carbs

In food processor with sharp blade or blender, or in bowl with electric mixer, process cream cheese until smooth.

In covered cereal bowl, microwave chocolate 2 minutes. Stir until melted. Add to cream cheese, along with Confectioner's Sugar Substitute, page 53, SPLENDA® Granular, whipping cream and vanilla extract. Process until smooth.

Place in 8-inch (20 cm) square glass baking dish. Cover with plastic wrap and press out evenly. Sprinkle pecan halves over top and press into surface. Refrigerate uncovered to keep pecans crisp.

Variation: **Chocolate Coconut Fudge:** Use $1^1/_2$ cups (375 mL) Confectioner's Sugar Substitute, page 53. Omit whipping cream and use 2 tbsp (25 mL) coconut oil, melted, instead. Add $^1/_2$ cup (125 mL) unsweetened desiccated coconut. Refrigerate. (*0.9 g Carbs*)

COOKIES & SQUARES

DELUXE CHOCOLATE CHIP COOKIES

Sensational, medium-sized chocolate chip cookies that rival the real thing!

$^3/_4$ cup unsalted butter, (175 mL)
  melted
$^3/_4$ cup light-tasting olive oil (175 mL)
2 eggs
1 tbsp vanilla extract (15 mL)
$2^1/_4$ cups SPLENDA® Granular (550 mL)
$2^1/_4$ cups Oat Ultimate Bake Mix (550 mL)
  OR Vital Oat Ultimate Bake Mix,
  page 67
2 cups quick-cooking oats (500 mL)
1 tsp baking powder (5 mL)
1 tsp baking soda (5 mL)
$^1/_2$ tsp salt (2 mL)
2 cups sugar free chocolate chips, (500 mL)
  (usually sweetened with a sugar alcohol)

Yield: 64 cookies
1 cookie
89.1 calories
2.0 g protein
8.0 g fat
2.6 g carbs

In food processor or blender, process butter, olive oil, eggs and vanilla extract. Add SPLENDA® Granular and process.

In large bowl, combine Oat Ultimate Bake Mix or Vital Oat Ultimate Bake Mix, page 67, quick-cooking oats, baking powder, baking soda and salt. Stir in wet ingredients. Fold in chocolate chips.

Drop level tablespoonfuls onto greased cookie sheets. Flatten with back of spoon. Bake in 375°F (190°C) oven 10 minutes.

Variations: **Hazelnut Cookies:** Omit sugar free chocolate chips. Add 2 cups (500 mL) chopped, blanched hazelnuts. Use Oat Ultimate Bake Mix or Vital Oat Ultimate Bake Mix, page 67, with ground hazelnuts. (***2.8 g Carbs***)

Raisin-Nut Cookies: Omit sugar free chocolate chips. Add $^1/_2$ cup (125 mL) raisins (snipped in half with scissors) and $1^1/_2$ cups (375 mL) chopped, blanched hazelnuts, almonds or pecans. (***3.7 g Carbs***)

BANANA ALMOND BUTTER COOKIES

Thick, soft cookies with a swirl of chocolate on top.

$^1/_2$ cup almond butter (125 mL)
$^1/_3$ cup mashed banana (75 mL)
$^1/_4$ cup butter, softened (50 mL)
1 egg
1 tsp vanilla extract (5 mL)
$1^1/_2$ cups Whey Ultimate (375 mL)
 Bake Mix, page 67
$^3/_4$ cup SPLENDA® Granular (175 mL)
2 tsp baking powder (10 mL)
$^1/_4$ tsp baking soda (1 mL)
$^1/_4$ tsp salt (1 mL)

Yield: 34 cookies
1 cookie
72.4 calories
2.7 g protein
5.6 g fat
3.2 g carbs

Topping:
$2^1/_2$ oz sugar free chocolate, (sweetened) (75 g)
$^1/_2$ tbsp butter (7 mL)
1 SPLENDA® packet

In food processor or electric mixer, process almond butter, mashed banana, butter, egg and vanilla extract.

In medium bowl, combine Whey Ultimate Bake Mix, page 67, SPLENDA® Granular, baking powder, baking soda and salt. Add to almond butter mixture and process briefly until combined. Use $1^1/_2$ tsp (7 mL) measuring spoon to help form into uniform balls. Flatten slightly with back of measuring spoon.

Bake in 350°F (180°C) oven 10 minutes, or until cookies are brown underneath. Allow to cool on rack. Garnish cookies with a swirl of chocolate.

Topping: In nonstick pan, melt chocolate and butter; stir in SPLENDA®.

Variation: **Banana Peanut Butter Cookies:** Use peanut butter instead of almond butter. (***3.1 g Carbs***)

NO BAKE CHOCOLATE COOKIES

A healthy, candy-like cookie.

1 cup quick-cooking oats (250 mL)
1 cup unsweetened coconut, (250 mL)
  finely desiccated
$1/4$ cup cocoa (50 mL)
10 SPLENDA® packets
2 tbsp whole OR skim milk (25 mL)
  powder
2 tbsp unsalted butter (25 mL)
2 tbsp peanut butter, no sugar or (25 mL)
  salt added, OR almond butter
$1/2$ cup Da Vinci® Sugar Free (125 mL)
  Chocolate Syrup
1 tsp vanilla extract (5 mL)

Yield: 24 cookies
1 cookie
57.6 calories
1.2 g protein
4.5 g fat
2.1 g carbs

In large bowl, combine oats, coconut, cocoa, SPLENDA® and whole or skim milk powder.

In cereal bowl, microwave butter and peanut butter or almond butter 1 minute. Stir in Da Vinci® Sugar Free Chocolate Syrup and vanilla extract.

Add peanut or almond butter mixture to dry ingredients, stirring until well combined.

Line cookie sheets with wax paper. Drop cookie dough by tablespoonfuls onto wax paper. Flatten with back of spoon. Refrigerate.

ALMOND BUTTER COOKIES

I think these may be one of the best almond cookies I have ever made.

$1^1/_2$ cup ground almonds (375 mL)
1 cup SPLENDA® Granular (250 mL)
$^1/_2$ cup almond butter, (125 mL)
 softened
2 extra-large eggs
1 tsp vanilla extract (5 mL)
$^1/_8$ tsp salt (0.5 mL)

Yield: 3 dozen cookies
1 plain cookie
40.4 calories
1.9 g protein
2.8 g fat
2.3 g carbs

In food processor or electric mixer, process ground almonds, SPLENDA® Granular, almond butter, eggs, vanilla and salt. Form dough into 1-inch (2.5 cm) smooth balls. Flatten with fork. Bake in 350°F (180°C) oven 13 minutes, or until brown underneath. Allow to cool on cookie sheet.

Variation: **Marzipan-flavored Cookies:** Add $^1/_8$ tsp (0.5 mL) almond extract and omit vanilla extract.

Almond Thumbprint Cookies: Roll into smooth balls. Press thumb or forefinger in middle of each cookie. Fill cooled cookie centers with Easy Berry Jam, page 58, or other low-carb fruit spread or Cinnamon Butter, page 59.

CHOCOLATE MACAROONS

High-fiber cookies. Not very sweet.

1 cup Crème Fraiche, page 54 (250 mL)
2 egg whites, fork beaten
1 tsp vanilla extract (5 mL)
$2^1/_2$ cups coconut, (625 mL)
 finely desiccated
$1^1/_2$ cups SPLENDA® Granular (375 mL)
2 tbsp Dutch cocoa (25 mL)

Yield: 58 macaroons
1 macaroon
39.9 calories
0.5 g protein
3.4 g fat
1.0 g carbs

In medium bowl, combine Crème Fraiche, page 54, egg whites and vanilla extract. In another medium bowl, combine coconut, SPLENDA® Granular and cocoa. Stir into Crème Fraiche mixture until well combined. Drop rounded teaspoons onto greased cookie sheets and bake in 325°F (160°C) oven 12 minutes.

ALMOND ROCO SQUARES

Very rich, very yummy! Quick and easy to prepare.

40 Snack Crackers (1 g carb ea.),
  each square 1.4 inches (3.5 cm)
  OR Flax Seed Crackers,* page 126
  Splendid Low-Carbing
$1^{1}/_{4}$ cups slivered almonds (300 mL)
$^{3}/_{4}$ cup butter, melted (175 mL)
1 tbsp whipping cream (15 mL) .
$^{1}/_{2}$ cup SPLENDA® Granular (125 mL)
1 cup sugar free chocolate chips, (250 mL)
  (sweetened, usually with a sugar alcohol)

Yield: 40 servings
1 serving
80.1 calories
1.4 g protein
7.4 g fat
2.3 g carbs

Line 9 x 13-inch (23 x 33 cm) glass baking dish with crackers, OR if using Flax Seed Crackers, page126, *Splendid Low-Carbing*, line with cracker dough and bake according to directions. Sprinkle almonds over crackers.

In medium bowl, combine cooled, melted butter, whipping cream and SPLENDA® Granular, in that order. Pour over crackers.

Bake in 350°F (180°C) oven 8 minutes. Remove and sprinkle with chocolate chips. Place in oven another 2 minutes. Draw tines of fork through molten chocolate in order to spread it. Cool before removing from baking dish to serve.

Helpful Hints: *If using Flax Seed Crackers, page 126, *Splendid Low-Carbing*, use just enough dough to comfortably cover the bottom of a greased 9 x 13-inch (23 x 33 cm) glass baking dish and bake. Cut into crackers as directed. Leave in pan and do not worry about any that break. Bake the rest of the cracker dough separately.

The original high-carb, sugar-filled recipe called for 1 cup (250 mL) of butter, making it extra rich and decadent, however, I think the amount indicated in the recipe is sufficiently decadent. Your family and friends will never guess these squares are low-carb.

SOUR CREAM BROWNIES

These very moist, sweet brownies become more dense and fudge-like after having been refrigerated a day or two.

2 cups SPLENDA® Granular (500 mL)
$^3/_4$ cup sour cream (175 mL)
$^1/_2$ cup unsalted butter, softened (125 mL)
$^1/_4$ cup Da Vinci® Sugar (50 mL)
  Free Chocolate Syrup
3 eggs
1 cup ground hazelnuts (250 mL)
$^1/_4$ cup chocolate whey protein (50 mL)
2 tbsp vital wheat gluten (25 mL)
$^1/_2$ tsp baking powder (2 mL)
$^1/_4$ tsp baking soda (1 mL)
2 oz baking chocolate (60 g)
  (unsweetened), melted
Chocolate Fudge Frosting, page 95

Yield: 36 squares
1 square
89.0 calories
2.3 g protein
8.0 g fat
2.8 g carbs

In food processor or in bowl using electric mixer, combine SPLENDA® Granular, sour cream, butter, Da Vinci® Sugar Free Chocolate Syrup and eggs. Process.

In medium bowl, combine hazelnuts, chocolate whey protein, vital wheat gluten, baking powder and baking soda. Add to first mixture; process. Add chocolate; process. Pour into well-greased 9-inch (23 cm) square glass baking dish.

Bake in 350°F (180°C) oven 35 to 40 minutes, or until cake tester inserted in center comes out clean. Add Frosting when cool and cut into squares.

Chocolate Fudge Frosting: Follow directions on page 95.

Variation: Da Vinci® Alternative: Use water and chocolate extract.

Helpful Hint: For slightly less moist brownies, use $^2/_3$ cup (150 mL) sour cream.

SESAME SNACKING SQUARES

Ian liked these solid, sweet, chewy squares packed with sesame seeds!

$1^1/_4$ cups sesame seeds (300 mL)
$^1/_2$ cup whole milk powder, (125 mL)
  OR skim milk powder
$^1/_2$ cup desiccated coconut, (125 mL)
  (unsweetened)
$^1/_2$ cup sugarless chocolate chips (125 mL)
4 SPLENDA® packets
$^1/_3$ cup almond butter (75 mL)
$^1/_4$ cup coconut oil (50 mL)

Yield: 36 squares	
1 square	
80.0 calories	
1.9 g protein	
7.4 g fat	
2.0 g carbs	

In large bowl, combine sesame seeds, whole or skim milk powder, coconut, chocolate chips and SPLENDA®. In small saucepan, heat almond butter and coconut oil, until coconut oil melts. Stir constantly. Do not worry if almond butter has not melted. Add to dry ingredients; stir. Chocolate should melt, if coconut oil is still very hot. Firmly pack in greased 9-inch (23 cm) square glass baking dish. Refrigerate until firm, and then cut into squares. Keep refrigerated.

ALMOND COCONUT SQUARES

A couple of these squares a day and there will be no need for pysillium husks!

$1^1/_2$ cups desiccated coconut, (375 mL)
  unsweetened
1 cup SPLENDA® Granular (250 mL)
$^1/_2$ cup almond butter (125 mL)
1-2 tbsp Da Vinci® Sugar (15-25 mL)
  Free Pancake Syrup, OR any other sugar
  free pancake syrup

Yield: 25 squares	
1 square	
75.8 calories	
1.1 g protein	
6.7 g fat	
2.2 g carbs	

In medium bowl, combine coconut, SPLENDA® Granular, almond butter and Da Vinci® Sugar Free Pancake Syrup. Press into greased 8-inch (20 cm) square glass baking dish. Refrigerate.

Variations: **Peanut Coconut Squares:** Use peanut butter instead of almond butter. (*2.0 g Carbs*). This version is not very sweet.

Lower Carb Alternative: Use 8 SPLENDA® packets. Almond Coconut Squares/Peanut Coconut Squares: (*1.5 g/1.3 g Carbs*)

CHOCOLATE SNOWFLAKE SQUARES

High fiber, chewy squares.

2 oz baking chocolate, (60 g)
  unsweetened
2 tbsp coconut oil, melted (25 mL)
16 SPLENDA® packets
$^1/_2$ cup chocolate whey protein (125 mL)
$^1/_2$ cup finely desiccated coconut (125 mL)
$^1/_4$ cup wheat bran (50 mL)
$^1/_4$ cup whole, OR skim milk (50 mL)
  powder
$^1/_4$ cup whipping cream (50 mL)
$^1/_4$ cup water (50 mL)
$^1/_3$ cup finely desiccated coconut (75 mL)
2 tbsp SPLENDA® Granular (25 mL)

Yield: 36 squares
1 square
46.4 calories
1.4 g protein
3.9 g fat
1.4 g carbs

In covered cereal bowl, microwave chocolate and coconut oil 2 minutes, until melted.

In medium bowl, mix SPLENDA®, chocolate whey protein, $^1/_2$ cup (125 mL) coconut, wheat bran and whole or skim milk powder. Stir in whipping cream and water. Stir in chocolate mixture.

In small bowl, combine $^1/_3$ cup (75 mL) coconut and SPLENDA® Granular. Sprinkle half coconut mixture in 8-inch (20 cm) square glass baking dish. Carefully spread chocolate dough over top of coconut, pressing out with back of spoon. Sprinkle remaining coconut over top. Refrigerate until firm.

Helpful Hints: Chill in freezer 20 minutes to hasten the hardening process, if desired.

2 cups (500 mL) SPLENDA® Granular may be used instead of the SPLENDA® packets. (***2.3 g Carbs***)

INDEX

CHICKEN ALFREDO IN CREPES 38
CHICKEN FAJITA IN A TACO 36
CHICKEN STRIPS WITH MEXI-CALI DIP 10
CHICKEN WRAP 36
CHOCOLATE ALMOND BUTTER CANDY 89
CHOCOLATE COCONUT FUDGE 98
CHOCOLATE CREAM POPSICLES 73
CHOCOLATE DRIZZLE 84
CHOCOLATE FUDGE FROSTING 95
CHOCOLATE MACAROONS 102
CHOCOLATE NUGGETS 98
CHOCOLATE PEANUT BUTTER CANDY 89
CHOCOLATE SHAKE 6
CHOCOLATE SNOWFLAKE SQUARES 106
CHUNKY TURKEY CHILI 37
CINNAMON BUTTER 59
CINNAMON RAISIN BREAD 70
CONDENSED MILK 56
CONFECTIONER'S SUGAR SUBSTITUTE 53

CONFECTIONS & FROSTINGS 89

CARAMEL PECAN FUDGE 97
CHOCOLATE ALMOND BUTTER CANDY 89
CHOCOLATE COCONUT FUDGE 98
CHOCOLATE DRIZZLE 84
CHOCOLATE FUDGE FROSTING 95
CHOCOLATE NUGGETS 98
CHOCOLATE PEANUT BUTTER CANDY 89
CREAM CHEESE FROSTING 65
CREAMY CHOCOLATE FROSTING 95
CREAMY TOFFEE 90
CREATE-A-FLAVOR CHOC. FROSTING 94
CREATE-A-FLAVOR CHOC. FUDGE 96
CREATE-A-FLAVOR PECAN FUDGE 97
CREATE-A-FLAVOR WHEY FROSTING 93
DARK CHOCOLATE ALMOND FUDGE 97
DOUBLE CHOCOLATE PROTEIN BARS 92
HAZELNUT CHOCOLATE FROSTING 94
MILK CHOCOLATE ALMOND FUDGE 97
RASPBERRY CHOCOLATE FROSTING 94
RASPBERRY CHOCOLATE FUDGE 96
RASPBERRY CHOCOLATE PROTEIN BARS 92
STRAWBERRY CHOC. PROTEIN BARS 92
TRUFFLES 90
VANILLA WHEY FROSTING 93
WHITE CHOCOLATE PECAN FUDGE 97
WHITE CHOCOLATE PROTEIN BARS 91

COOKIES & SQUARES 99

ALMOND BUTTER COOKIES 102
ALMOND COCONUT SQUARES 105
ALMOND ROCO SQUARES 103
ALMOND THUMBPRINT COOKIES 102
BANANA ALMOND BUTTER COOKIES 100
BANANA PEANUT BUTTER COOKIES 100
CHOCOLATE MACAROONS 102
CHOCOLATE SNOWFLAKE SQUARES 106
DELUXE CHOCOLATE CHIP COOKIES 99
HAZELNUT COOKIES 99
MARZIPAN-FLAVORED COOKIES 102

NO BAKE CHOCOLATE COOKIES 101
PEANUT COCONUT SQUARES 105
RAISIN-NUT COOKIES 99
SESAME SNACKING SQUARES 105
SOUR CREAM BROWNIES 104
CRANBERRY ORANGE LOAF 66
CRANBERRY-PECAN MUFFINS 63
CREAM CHEESE BRAN WAFFLES 20
CREAM CHEESE FLAP JACKS 21
CREAM CHEESE FROSTING 65
CREAM-ON-TOP JELLY 76
CREAMY CHOCOLATE FROSTING 95
CREAMY TOFFEE 90
CREATE-A-FLAVOR CHOC. FROSTING 94
CREATE-A-FLAVOR CHOC. FUDGE 96
CREATE-A-FLAVOR FROZEN YOGURT 78
CREATE-A-FLAVOR ICED TEA 5
CREATE-A-FLAVOR JELLY 76
CREATE-A-FLAVOR MUFFIN 62
CREATE-A-FLAVOR PECAN FUDGE 97
CREATE-A-FLAVOR PIE 82
CREATE-A-FLAVOR POPSICLE 73
CREATE-A-FLAVOR SHAKE 6
CREATE-A-FLAVOR SWEET BUTTER 59
CREATE-A-FLAVOR WHEY FROSTING 93
CREATE-A-FLAVOR YOGURT ICE CREAM 72
CRÈME FRAICHE 54
CROCK-POT BEEF ROAST 26
CRUNCHY GRANOLA 22
CURRIED FRUITED PORK 33

D

DARK CHOCOLATE ALMOND FUDGE 97
DELUXE CHOCOLATE CHIP COOKIES 99
DIJON SALMON FILLETS 44
DOUBLE CHOCOLATE PROTEIN BARS 92
DOUBLE CHOCOLATE WHIRL 74

E

EASY BERRY JAMS 58
EASY RHUBARB CRUMBLE 75
EGGPLANT ALMONDINE 49
EGGPLANT LASAGNA 47
EXOTIC AVOCADO MOLD 15

F

FAUX BAKED POTATO SOUP 18
FAUX BLUEBERRY OATMEAL 25

FISH & SHELLFISH 41

BAKED LOBSTER TAILS 44
DIJON SALMON FILLETS 44

ORDERING INFORMATION
(All Prices below include S&H via USPS media mail)

SPLENDID LOW-CARBING **$24** US

MORE SPLENDID LOW-CARBING **$17** US

SPLENDID LOW-CARBING FOR LIFE (Volume-1) **$17** US

Or <u>all 3</u> **"SPLENDID LOW-CARBING" cookbooks** $55 US

Also, you can still order **SPLENDID DESSERTS** **$13** US

And **MORE SPLENDID DESSERTS** **$15** US

Or order <u>Both of these</u> **"SPLENDID DESSERTS" cookbooks** $26 US

Any/All of these books can be ordered by MAIL simply by
sending your selections and a check, money order or bank draft to:

Aurum Group
PO Box 907,
Great Falls, MT
USA 59403
BUT, p*lease allow 4-8 weeks for delivery when ordering by mail!*

Or *save money* and get these books much sooner by ordering <u>SECURELY</u> online from:
www.sweety.com or www.Low-Carb.us *Also look for this "Splendid" series of
cookbooks to be available through **Amazon.com***'s very popular website.*

Please note: Recipes in *Splendid Desserts* and *More Splendid Desserts* can now be
adapted to suit a low-carb lifestyle by using your choice of Ultimate Bake Mix on page
67 or 68 or by requesting a copy of these recipes. As well, any "special order" inquiries
can be sent to the above address or emailed to **Desserts@Sweety.com**

---

(1) Although I have satisfied myself concerning the safety of SPLENDA$^{®}$, it is up to each individual to decide that independently. For more information on the safety of SPLENDA$^{®}$ Low-Calorie Sweetener, call 1-800-561-0070 in Canada or write to SPLENDA$^{®}$ Information Center, P.O. Box 1390, Guelph, Ontario, Canada N1K 1A5, or in the U.S.A. write to SPLENDA$^{®}$ Information Center, 501 George Street, JH305, New Brunswick, NJ, USA 08901.

(2) SPLENDA$^{®}$ Low-Calorie Sweetener is the registered trademark of McNeil-PPC, Inc. Neither McNeil Specialty Products nor McNeil Consumer Products Company have been involved in the development, production or distribution of this cookbook.

(3) Da Vinci$^{®}$ Gourmet is the registered trademark of Da Vinci Gourmet, Ltd. They have not been involved in the development or production of this cookbook.